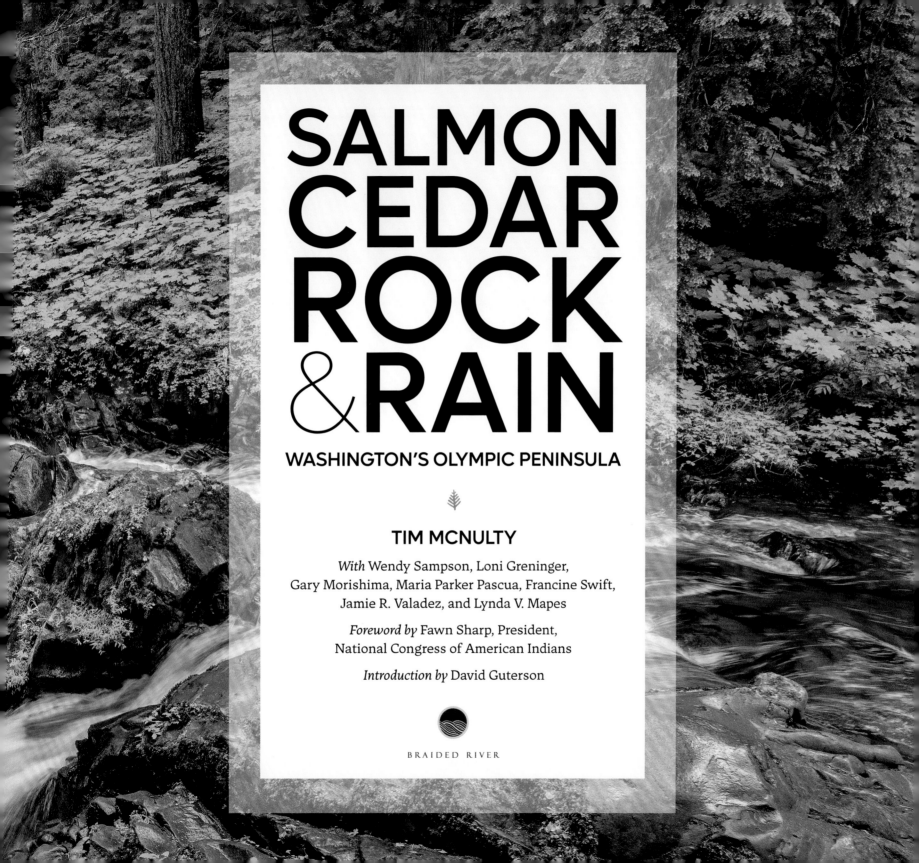

# SALMON CEDAR ROCK & RAIN

## WASHINGTON'S OLYMPIC PENINSULA

**TIM MCNULTY**

*With* Wendy Sampson, Loni Greninger,
Gary Morishima, Maria Parker Pascua, Francine Swift,
Jamie R. Valadez, and Lynda V. Mapes

*Foreword by* Fawn Sharp, President,
National Congress of American Indians

*Introduction by* David Guterson

BRAIDED RIVER

The publisher and all the contributors to *Salmon, Cedar, Rock & Rain* respectfully acknowledge that this book celebrates the lands of Indigenous Peoples who have resided in and cared for these places since time immemorial.

We recognize and honor the treaty rights for each tribe: Hoh Tribe, Jamestown S'Klallam Tribe, Lower Elwha Klallam Tribe, Makah Tribe, Port Gamble S'Klallam Tribe, Quileute Tribe, Quinault Indian Nation, and Skokomish Indian Tribe.

We are grateful for both their ancestral and current stewardship of the Olympic Peninsula's lands, as well as their generosity in sharing stories and images that embrace its forests, mountains, and waters.

**Streamside trees are reflected in the Hoko River along Hoko-Ozette Road.**

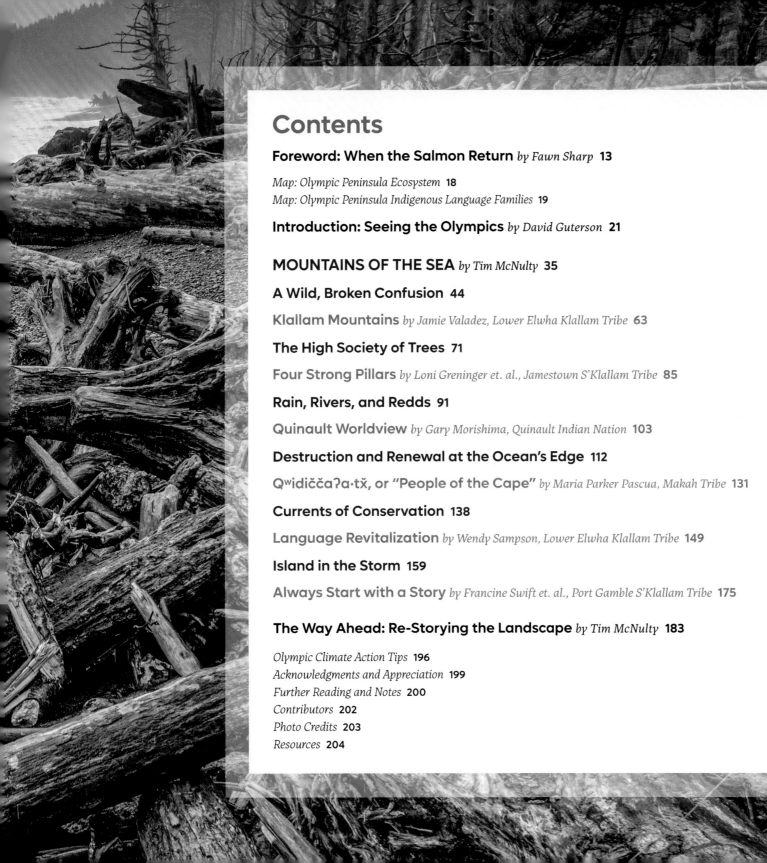

# Contents

Coho salmon migrate up the Sol Duc River. Coho navigate some 50 miles of the Sol Duc and climb Salmon Cascades before spawning in quiet waters in Olympic National Park.

# Foreword: When the Salmon Return

**FAWN SHARP**

If one were to describe Heaven on Earth, one might conjure an image of the Olympic Peninsula. As a Native who oversees the largest tribal organization in the United States, I have seen many places and experienced breathtaking vistas and environs both near and far. There is no doubt we live in a beautiful country—and Tribes across the continent should be credited for helping to keep it that way.

Every time I return home from my travels, I am treated to the most incredible land of all. It's where great herds of Roosevelt elk abound; where black bear wander in search of ripe huckleberries; and where mammals, from wild goats to marmots, enjoy life in bountiful forests. It's where birds of many species dart through the sky and build their nests in stately evergreen trees or on our many coastlines. Ours is a land of majestic mountains and clear, blue lakes. Streams and rivers rush from the mountains to the sea, providing a home for five species of our icon, the great Pacific Salmon: Chinook, sockeye, steelhead, pink, and chum. They all return to our rivers and lakes after traveling thousands of miles in the Pacific.

But the salmon are not returning in the numbers they should. A keystone species where I live, their lives support the very existence of many native animals and plants, just as they support the lives of our people, from the time they hatch in the gravels of our rivers to the time of their return as adults. As the habitat that sustains the salmon wanes, however, so too do their numbers. When climate change warms the ocean and our inland waters, when it causes severe storms, landslides, droughts, sea level rise, glacial loss, floods, and other damage, it kills salmon. There are other causes of salmon decline—often including non-tribal activities that violate treaties—but whatever the cause, the impact on our ecosystem is significant. Our fishermen are suffering, but we can only open our fisheries when the salmon return in adequate numbers and the escapement (the number that can be

Ocean bluffs and islands line the unspoiled coastline north of Pratt Cliff on the Quinault Indian Reservation.

accommodated by available habitat) is adequate to sustain the resource. The opportunity to fish is far more rare than it should be, especially with naturally spawning fish.

It has been said that the salmon will return when we all work as hard to protect them as they do to reach their spawning grounds—so we need to come together to protect and restore their natural habitat. Increased funding can be used to support our fisheries departments. It can be used to acquire habitat, plant trees, fight wildfires, and protect water resources. But it's not enough. People from all walks of life need to learn they have a stake here. Everyone needs to support clean air and water like never before. Whether through political pressure or volunteerism, we all need to rise up and support habitat protection, clean energy, and accurate education about the relationship we all have with the environment. All of us need to set good examples—keep poisonous substances from entering our watersheds, conserve power and water, drive electric and hybrid cars, recycle, become more educated about environmental issues. We all have a stake and we all have responsibilities. Together, we can bring the salmon home.

When I get to my home on magnificent Lake Quinault and report to my duties at Quinault Indian Nation, I feel overwhelmed with happiness, relief, and pure joy. I realize we Quinaults are among the small number of Americans who can walk the same beaches, paddle the same waters, and hunt the same lands our ancestors did centuries ago. Located on the southwestern corner of the Olympic Peninsula, our rain-drenched lands embrace an immense variety of natural resources; we have sovereign jurisdiction over thousands of acres of unspoiled coastlines and some of the most productive conifer forests in the entire country, including one of the country's last remaining rain forests.

Often, however, I also feel deep sadness. I feel the burden of decades of environmental genocide when I am reminded that those natural resources no longer exist in the numbers they once did. It is heartbreaking to see our salmon returns dwindle so substantially. But tribal leaders cannot afford to wallow in negative emotions. We have to be positive in our efforts to make things better and keep hope alive. We have to keep working to meet the needs of our people on a

sustainable basis. We have to do whatever is necessary to protect our culture and heritage, to protect the future of our youth and help our people be all they can be.

We have long realized that we are not alone in these efforts. That is why we support books such as this and welcome the efforts of such organizations as The Mountaineers and Braided River. It's why we reach out to form coalitions, welcome people to visit the beautiful Olympic Peninsula, and learn from their experiences. And when you do visit, please remember to treat our traditional land with respect. Love it, but don't love it to death. Then, when you return to your homes, please take the time to teach others how they can help preserve our wildlands and unique natural resources.

You, too, can help forge the way to a better tomorrow.

The Tlingit canoe *Dzunugwungis* and paddlers arrive in the south bay of Point Grenville during the 2013 intertribal Paddle to Quinault. The tall ship *Lady Washington* sails in the background.

TOP **A Quinault tribal member digs for razor clams in evening light south of Point Grenville on the Quinault Indian Reservation.**
BOTTOM **A Quinault redcedar canoe and paddlers head out to sea from the cove at Point Grenville on the start of a canoe journey.**
OPPOSITE **Contemporary Quinault crafts embrace timeless traditions: woven baskets that hold razor clams, a cedar-bark mat, and a decorative Japanese fishing float cover with an intricate whale design.**

# Olympic Peninsula Ecosystem

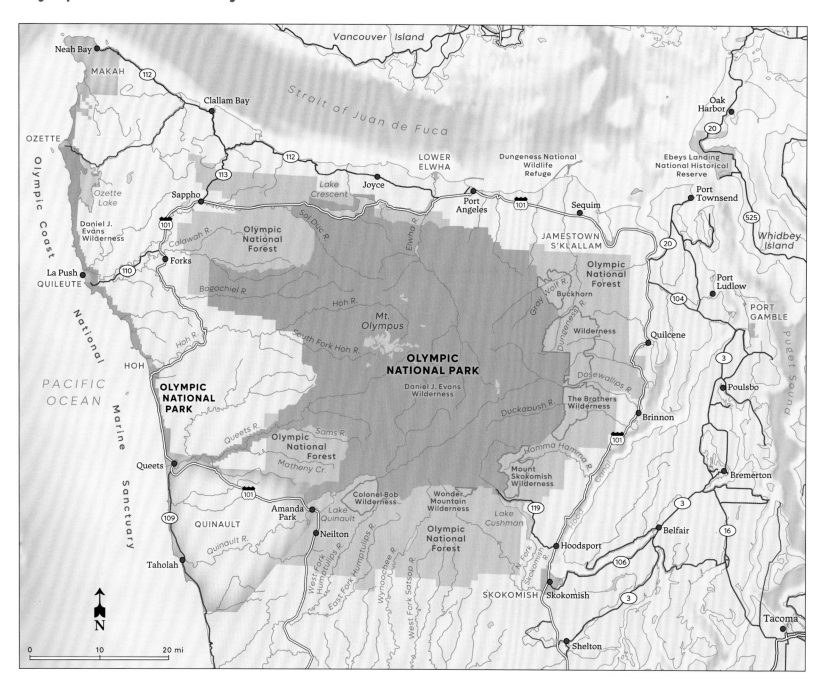

# Olympic Peninsula Indigenous Language Families

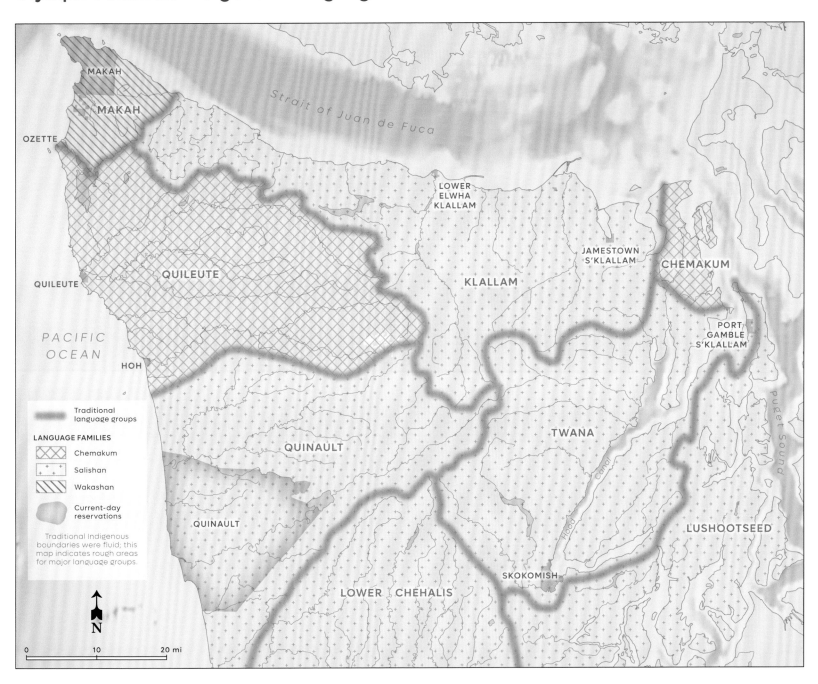

MAKAH

MAKAH

OZETTE

Strait of Juan de Fuca

LOWER
ELWHA
KLALLAM

JAMESTOWN
S'KLALLAM

CHEMAKUM

QUILEUTE

QUILEUTE

KLALLAM

PORT
GAMBLE
S'KLALLAM

PACIFIC
OCEAN

HOH

TWANA

QUINAULT

Traditional
language groups

LANGUAGE FAMILIES

Chemakum

Salishan

Wakashan

Current-day
reservations

Traditional Indigenous
boundaries were fluid; this
map indicates rough areas
for major language groups.

QUINAULT

L'USHOOTSEED

SKOKOMISH

LOWER   CHEHALIS

Puget Sound

Hood Canal

N

0        10        20 mi

One of the most stunning views in the Olympics: the High Divide and the Mount Olympus massif rise above the fog-shrouded Hoh Valley in Olympic National Park.

# Introduction: Seeing the Olympics

**DAVID GUTERSON**

I plan on getting to the territory of this book, but first, bear with me and take a look at your right hand, palm down. You'll notice, among other things, that your thumb appears distant from your other fingers, which all point north, so to speak, and extend in parallel. Aloof and awry, rooted in the west and rotated out, your thumb looks isolated, solitary, peninsular.

Florida, which you can easily see in your mind's eye as a thumb, is obviously peninsular. No one looking at a map of the United States can fail to notice Florida's thumb-like shape and that it's surrounded by water on three sides. By comparison, the peninsula of interest in this book—the Olympic Peninsula in Washington state—is vague on a map, easy to miss.

Maps, though, can be misleading. A common one depicts the contiguous United States as if it were divorced from Canada, Mexico, and both adjoining oceans, none of which are represented. This allows viewers to focus their attention on the names and positions of the states (Alaska and Hawaii are marooned in sidebars), but it also encourages a false view of reality. No, Maine is not a peninsula. In fact, it's the opposite—Maine is surrounded on three sides by land. Meanwhile, Michigan's Upper Peninsula suffers the opposite fate in map depictions by nearly butting up against Canada. In the first case, something that isn't a peninsula appears to be one; in the second, something that is gets lost.

Sometimes peninsulas defy what we imagine. They're supposed to be dead ends of a sort, yet you can drive to the far end of the Upper Peninsula and then, via a bridge, keep going. The same is true of the Delmarva Peninsula, which after playing out southward allows access to Virginia via bridge and tunnel both, letting Philadelphians skirt the traffic in Baltimore and DC. Peninsulas like these are exceptions, though. Most are on the way to nowhere. You don't pass through them on a journey to somewhere else, and eventually you'll have to turn around to leave. As such, they're either destinations or missed. You're either going to one or not. On the Olympic Peninsula, for example, a traveler is ultimately stopped by Cape Flattery, the northwesternmost point in the contiguous United States. After that, more than four thousand miles away, lies Kamchatka.

Take in your right hand again. This time, bend your fingers until only the parts where rings are worn show. You can even bend your thumb a little if you want, giving it a more northward cast. The shape you're looking at now is loosely akin to that of the state of Washington. That V-shaped gap between your thumb and the bulk of your hand represents the gap between the Olympic Peninsula and the rest of the state. This gap is rarely clear on maps. It looks trivial. Scale obscures its meaning. Your right hand in silhouette, arranged as prescribed, does a better job of telling you about the distance between the Olympic Peninsula and everything else.

**I'M FROM SEATTLE. I WAS BORN THERE AND HAVE** lived in or near it for all but nine months of my life. I answer the question, "Where do you live?" with, "Near Seattle"; abroad I sometimes feel driven to add, "In Washington, the state, in the west, not Washington, DC." Plenty of people I meet, though, know where Seattle is, albeit sometimes just approximately. "You're on the Pacific," they might say to me (before adding, "I hear it rains a lot").

Actually, Seattle isn't on the Pacific. In fact, it's not even close. If you want to get to the Pacific from Seattle—about ninety miles west of the city as the crow flies—you have to drive for at least two and a half hours. Circuitously, conspicuously so, and via a route much longer than a crow's.

Why is that? It's because due west of Seattle lies Puget Sound, a north-south arm of the Salish Sea encompassing just over a thousand square miles, and because west of that lies another north-south arm of the Salish Sea known as Hood Canal (though it's no canal), and because west of both is the Olympic Peninsula, a 3,600-square-mile mountainous bulwark. This means first, two saltwater crossings, and second, mountains through which no roads make their way to the coast.

Mountains, you would think, aren't barriers to traffic, because they rear up in ranges cut by passes; you can drive through the Rockies, for example, or the Appalachians, on interstate freeways. Not the Olympics. They

don't constitute a range. They're arrayed, instead, as a proliferation, and they are as thick with mountains north to south as they are east to west. They form a density, so that in the end you have to drive around them if you want to get to the ocean from Seattle in a car. It's a long drive, but well worth the time, because like much of the peninsula's mountainous terrain, much of the coast lies within Olympic National Park and is untrammeled by development.

To summarize: the peninsula under consideration in this book is piled high with mountains no road crosses. Its forests are dense. Its most trafficked highway is mostly a two-lane road. Towns there are few and far between.

**THERE IS, AT BEST, ONLY A MODEST LITERATURE OF** the Olympic Peninsula, by which I mean, in this case, a literature that allows for the contemplation of qualities peculiar to it. Its urtext, maybe, emerged in 1955—a wide-ranging, informal, and anecdotal history written by a journalist named Murray Morgan. Morgan's title, *The Last Wilderness*, is both apt and telling because this quality of "last," or of the end of something, doggedly adheres to the Olympic Peninsula, and not just because it's land's end in the Pacific Northwest. Equally salient, I think, is that when Morgan wrote, swaths of the peninsula still hung on as "wilderness"—a notion that ignores its most enduring inhabitants—whereas the rest of the country's was gone and missed. By the early 1990s, when William Dietrich's *The Final Forest* limned the battle between loggers and environmentalists over the last of the peninsula's old-growth trees, a lot had changed, but as Dietrich's title suggests, an aura of finality still clung to the place. The same holds today, three decades later. Lose this, the Olympic Peninsula continues to suggest, and something's finished.

But one person's final forest is another's frontier. Where one person sees wilderness, another sees profit. That's why Thomas T. Aldwell's *Conquering the Last Frontier* can sit on the same bookshelf as Murray Morgan's *The Last*

Old-growth Douglas-fir, their tops lost in fog, grow to heights approaching 250 feet in the rain-saturated valleys of the Olympic Mountains. Douglas-fir seedlings sprout in open ground following natural disturbances—or logging—and can grow for centuries.

*Wilderness*. Both are about the Olympic Peninsula, both appeared in the 1950s, and both purport to be about something "last," but in the end these titles oppose one another like flip sides of the same coin. There are clear reasons for this. Morgan was a journalist of varied interests, sardonic when it came to human nature and progress. Aldwell, by contrast, was a businessman who, near the end of his life, chronicled his contributions to conquering the frontier

he'd found—or formulated for himself—on the Olympic Peninsula's Elwha River.

"The frontier" is a concept that can also mean "invasion." Americans long ago fell in love with the idea, to the point that our nation became entangled with the term: one Oxford English Dictionary definition of "frontier" includes, for example, that it especially refers "to the western US before Pacific settlement." "Frontier," of course, suggests

The Elwha Dam, powerhouse, and spillway were constructed in 1913. The Elwha and later the Glines Canyon dams blocked salmon from more than seventy miles of pristine spawning habitat. Both dams were removed by 2014, and salmon are once more returning to the Elwha River.

the front of something—in the case of the United States, the front of something moving west—without, at the same time, acknowledging this implication: that as something presses forward, something else retreats, or that as one thing is gained, another's lost. About this I don't mean to be binary, because what's wilderness for some is home for others, and what was the frontier for American explorers and pioneers was, for the people already there, the leading edge of an inundation. There are, then, more than two choices, and many ways of looking at the same thing.

In *Conquering the Last Frontier*, Aldwell records for posterity his efforts to dam the Elwha. Inexorably, his dream dam is realized, and the lake backed up behind it, 270 acres broad and 94 feet deep, is given his name. Later, upriver, another dam goes in and is named for one of Aldwell's business partners; the lake behind that one is named for their associate, the founder of a peninsula forest products company. *Conquering the Last Frontier* chronicles all of this without noting that, when Lake Aldwell filled, it inundated the Klallam people's place of genesis, the site where, according to their religious tradition, their Creator made them. For them, the vicinity of what became Lake Aldwell wasn't wilderness, last or otherwise, nor was it something to be transmuted into profit. It was instead a holy place, erased now without compunction, unknown and nameless to its usurpers.

**THOMAS T. ALDWELL CAME TO THE OLYMPIC PENIN-**sula in 1890, the same year its mountains began to be surveyed; before that they appeared on maps as a blank space meant to indicate the unknown. To put this lack of knowledge in context, in 1890 forty-two thousand people lived in Seattle, where the Olympics were readily visible on clear days. Also, the United States began that year to use tabulating machines to process census punch cards, the first winged aircraft took off under its own power in France, the London Tube opened, the jukebox was invented, and Sequoia and Yosemite National Parks were established. To

repeat: all of this was concurrent with the first survey of the Olympics, undertaken ten years before the twentieth century began. Until it was completed and maps were produced, the place provoked a lot of cliche and hyperbole, as in "shrouded in mystery" and "cloaked in mist." The Olympics, wrote Washington Territory's last governor, were "like a realization of a dream of the resurrection; as if they had been in the grave and had come forth clad in the robes of innocence to a command of Jehovah . . . you can imagine them to be the walls of paradise, enclosing scenes of bliss."

The territorial era soon ended, but not the cliché and hyperbole. In 1889, Washington State's first governor compared the Olympics to "the interior of Africa," a "great unknown land" where, he was convinced, no one had set foot. This situation, he felt, should be remedied, and soon. Forthwith, the necessary funding materialized. By the end of the following year no fewer than ten expeditions had been mounted and the Olympic Mountains had largely been mapped—a practical gain, but a loss of enchantment.

Maps, ironically, can restrict our comprehension of what they represent. Mostly they depict the world as if from an altitude experienced only by astronauts. Today their accuracy is essentially total, which has made them more useful than they used to be, while at the same time solidifying their hold on our way of knowing where we are in the world. More than once, though, I've tried to imagine how people found their way before cartographic maps, particularly in the view-throttled domain of the Olympic rain forest. Certainly they made use of knowledge, when available, passed by word of mouth. They also followed trails made by animals, elk in particular. If possessed of the relevant intimate experience—if the rain forest was familiar as, and felt to be, home—then subtle contours, gradations of flora, changes in river sound, and the moods of the light as it pierced the canopy were all as good as or better than a map. Immersed in this way, without a view from the stratosphere—what way of seeing, of being, did they inhabit? What did it mean for their feelings about the world?

A QUALITY OF TARDINESS—OF A LAND THAT SLEPT late (to borrow from the title of Robert L. Wood's book about the place)—was imposed on the Olympic Peninsula at about the same time it became, depending on who you ask, a last wilderness or a last frontier. In this view, things happened there in dilatory fashion, every event a step or two behind. The peninsula was a kind of straggler, but charmed, slightly out of step while lagging.

The first European explorers to go ashore on the peninsula did so in 1775 (or so records suggest), at a time when over two million people had already colonized North America's eastern seaboard. Westering migrants, too, came "late" to the peninsula—late, that is, relative to those pioneers who galvanized en masse and trooped across the plains in the first half of the nineteenth century, but neither early nor late to the people living on the peninsula when they arrived. For that matter, "pioneer" is up for grabs as a term with settled meaning.

The migrants who found their way to the peninsula did so—from within their own frame of reference—well after the main thrust of American pioneering had co-opted the plains, well after barbed wire had carved up western ranges, well after gold had brought hordes to California, and well after Oregon Country was transformed into farmland. This meant that the mythos of American settlement remained available on the peninsula on the cusp of the twentieth century, when and where it in fact took hold, albeit in a more rain-addled form than the varieties generated on the Great Plains or in the basins and sage lands of the intermontane West. Intrepid undertakings and muscular refusal to be bested by nature—the staple fare of American settler mythology—were suffused on the peninsula with forest gloom and heavy rain, its characters saturated, sodden, and clammy, if occasionally brightened by a mountaintop interlude marked by sunlit views in all directions. In a place like that, a westering soul could feel psychic impulses flow in two directions. On the one hand, dark forests, unnerving and silent, seeped in as if eternally harboring the demonic. On the other, lofty mountains intimated transcendence. Early Olympic Peninsula explorers and settlers were subject to these polar forces. It took a peculiar sort of person, really, to want to be there at all, in a place where sentimentality had little use and a romantic view of nature even less.

The Olympic Peninsula didn't lend itself to romantic treatment by its settlers. Romantics, after all, feed on the luminous; these settlers had chosen the gloomy and claustrophobic. Romantics exalt the "sublime" and "transcendent"; these settlers settled amid desultory rains. Romantics despair at the loss of nature; these settlers saw it as mostly in their way. They were more stoic than anything else—that is, romantic about themselves to the point of pretending not to be. Frequently the result was a "less is more" persona, plain speaking and understated. At the same time, the notes, journals, diaries, and memoirs generated by the new denizens of the Olympic Peninsula were constructed to suggest that good cheer was infallible for them, and that the monumental tasks of their lives were no big deal. If you wanted to see them as Bunyanesque, you were going to have to read between the lines (which is where they were pointing you). In fact, they seemed to want to outdo each other in making little of strenuous exploits. It's as if without a rigorous modesty and a straight face, none of it counted.

The anecdotes produced by narrators of this sort are a pleasure to come across, and ultimately winning, offering as they do improbable feats about which they demur with a wink. (LeRoy Smith, in *Pioneers of the Olympic Peninsula*, reports that Tom Newton "climbed a spruce tree one Sunday, about two hundred feet, cut all the limbs going up, and put a little windmill on top that ran for several years." Next sentence: "Tom, Scott Iverson, Gus and I fished the Calawah River about every Sunday.") They suggest a culture of idiosyncratic mavericks, of people who not only couldn't take civilization but had a problem, too, with taking ease. In some ways they were simply pioneers who, having been born too late to star in the main drama, were writing its sequel in the last place available, with themselves cast in central roles they felt self-conscious about. In other ways they were members of that subcategory of pioneers who

In early fall as rutting season begins, bull elk gather "harems" of females and defend them against other male contenders. Olympic National Park protects the largest unmanaged population of Roosevelt elk in the United States.

A flurry of bigleaf maple leaves falls over the lower Elwha River as seen from the Elwha River Pedestrian Bridge on the Olympic Discovery Trail.

were less pioneers than nonconformists and dissenters, offbeat and irrepressible, freedom seeking and indomitable. They endured, with apparent happiness, rain-soaked and rudimentary American lives on the cusp of the twentieth century, and well into it too, largely by choice. In this regard they were their own brand of romantic—rain-soaked, maybe, but romantics nonetheless.

SPEAKING OF ROMANTICS, ROBERT L. WOOD BEGINS his *Olympic Mountains Trail Guide* with an epigraph from William Wordsworth:

. . . The sounding cataract
Haunted me like a passion; the tall rock,
The mountain, and the deep and gloomy wood,
Their colors and their forms, were then to me
An appetite; a feeling and a love,
That had no need of a remoter charm,
By thoughts supplied, nor any interest
Unborrowed from the eye.

Reading Wood, the author of six books about the Olympics—including three histories of exploration—I'm at times reminded that he worked as a stenographer, pecking away at a steno machine in the service of trial transcripts while seated in a courtroom, a job far removed from the places that haunted him like a passion (in particular Mount Olympus, which he climbed eighteen times). This might be why his *Olympic Mountains Trail Guide* has, at least for me, a quality of poignant yearning.

My copy of Wood's trail guide is about as battered, chewed, dog-eared, and unglued as a book can get. Wood is sometimes purple and for long stretches disinterested in his prose, and his figures of speech can be ill-chosen ("On hot afternoons walking from the sun-drenched meadows into the shaded coolness of the forest is almost like entering an air-conditioned home in the desert"), but he's also, in my case, easy to forgive, because the sounding Olympic cataract haunts me like a passion, too. I've carried him as a voice in my head over many miles and many years, so that

for better or worse I've been permeated by his guidance ("At Eleven Bull Basin, the hiker has a choice: keep low beneath Stephen Peak, more or less contouring to Cream Lake, or climb up and over the peak, perhaps descending to Stephen Lake to camp"). Wood sometimes sits on my shoulder like a homunculus intoning fussy prescriptions, but he's also been a soother of doubts, a reliable source of confirmation, a verifier of observations, and essential to me as a fount of specifics. He's been right so many times about so many things that my faith in his assertions has become absolute. For me, Wood is the old map, pre-cartography, the one transmitted down the years in raw language. "I do not know how many miles I have walked in these mountains," he writes, "but it must number in the thousands." Which means he's earned the right to his romantic digressions, like the ones in the final paragraph of his guidebook. "The snowy peaks change quickly from white to rosy pink, then red, and finally lavender and purple as the shadows creep up from the deep canyons," Wood writes of a sunset witnessed from the top of Mount Olympus. "The day breaks bright, clear, and cold, with fog in the low valleys, clouds in the distance," he writes of dawn on the same summit. There is really no guidance in any of that other than to look through his eyes, which I don't find off-putting. We are, after all, creatures of cultures, and therefore subject from the beginning of our lives to the languages of forebears and to historical circumstance. Yet our sensibilities can evolve, too. We can look beyond the angles of our moment. Our looking can be both forward and back—back along a line through time to others who've loved the places we love, and forward toward those who will one day ponder you and me, their ancestors.

**Prominent in the eastern Olympics, peaks in The Brothers Wilderness in Olympic National Forest rise sharply above the lowlands of Hood Canal and Puget Sound.**

A great blue heron takes off from its fertile feeding grounds within an eelgrass bed exposed at low tide in Dungeness Bay.

At 7,756 feet in elevation, snowy Mount Constance anchors the view of the eastern Olympic Mountains from Puget Sound and Seattle while fog and shadow dampen the lowlands.

The Brothers in dawn light

# MOUNTAINS OF THE SEA

## TIM MCNULTY

Two ebony cormorants shot like winged darts across the bow, and gulls glided lazily over the upper deck as the ferry *Hyak* thrummed across the luminescent waters of the Puget Sound. The Seattle skyline grew small behind me, its glass towers lit by the setting sun. Before me the rough-hewn crags of the Olympic Mountains rose blue and snowcapped in the flushed glow of the sky. This was my first long-awaited look at the Olympic Peninsula, the culmination of a summer cross-country hitchhiking trip. Although it was more than fifty years ago, the image remains imprinted in my imagination. In the years since, this wild, wooded, river-carved corner of the Pacific Northwest has become a home for me and a focus of my work as a writer and conservationist. Of course, I knew nothing of that back then. What I remember most vividly is the flush of excitement that accompanied that first glimpse of the mountains; it prickled my skin and kept me out on the windy deck long after my fellow passengers had retreated to the warmth of the cabin.

From Puget Sound, the Olympic Mountains rise abruptly from saltwater shores and forested foothills as if adrift in a shallow sea. In many ways, the ocean defines the Olympic Peninsula; its restless floor gave birth to the mountains and coastal lowlands, and a perpetual river of moist marine air sustains its stunning profusion of life. The nearness of the mountains to the sea completes the cycle. The prominent 7,743-foot summit of Mount Constance looms only a dozen miles from the saltwater shore of Quilcene Bay; 6,454-foot Mount Angeles is a mere ten miles from Port Angeles Harbor. Surrounded by water—the

Pacific Ocean to the west, the enfolding arms of the Salish Sea to the north and east, and the low valley of the Chehalis River to the south—the peninsula is nearly an island. For extended periods in its geological past, it *was* an island, and that legacy is reflected in the character and diversity of plant and animal communities that thrive here today. The peninsula's dense cluster of snowcapped peaks with their wet-side/dry-side ecologies and its radiating network of watersheds heading in mountain glaciers and snowfields and streaming to inlets, bays, and rocky beaches comprise a land self-contained and apart from the nearby mainland.

Geographically, culturally, and historically, the peninsula is a territory unto itself. Its isolation is part of its mystique, and for much of the past two centuries it may have been its saving grace. Mount Olympus, recorded by Spanish explorer Juan Pérez in 1774 as the "Snowy Peak of Saint Rosalia," was the first feature to be named in what would become Washington state, but its surrounding mountains were the last to be explored and mapped by Euro-Americans in the lower 48.

From long before Captain Pérez and the wooden ships of conquest and commerce, the peninsula remains home to its original people. Eight sovereign tribes maintain traditional homelands on the peninsula. Indigenous people have dwelled here and cared for this place since time immemorial, time beyond memory. Evidence of human presence on the peninsula dates back to a time when remnants of Ice Age glaciers lingered in the foothills and mastodon and bison roamed the emerging lowlands—a time when the earth, in a very human sense, was new. Nourished by the bounty of the land, rivers, and sea, Northwest Coast people developed some of the most refined and sophisticated cultures in North America. The archaeological sites of Ozette and Tse-whit-zen villages offer glimpses into complex cultures exquisitely adapted to their environments. With the arrival of Pérez and others, the timeless continuity of human life on the peninsula underwent profound change. Russia, Spain, Great Britain, and the United States vied for control of the newly "discovered" land and its relatively untouched trove of resources.

The eighteenth and early nineteenth centuries brought fur trappers, traders, and seafarers to the peninsula's shores. None stayed. When the United States boundary was finally established along the Strait of Juan de Fuca in 1846, not a single white settler inhabited the peninsula. But soon after, timber barons, cannery operators, and land speculators washed ashore in waves. Town sites, shipping ports, and sawmills took hold on the peninsula, and schemes for railroads linking it to the mainland soon followed. As the homesteading era drew to a close in America, this "last frontier" offered the promise of land, independence, and self-determination. Homesteaders, including many immigrants to the United States, sought opportunities to carve new lives out of the endless forests. Settlers ploughed the native prairies, miners pecked away at the hills, and lumbermen hewed sizable domains out of the coastal forests. Populations boomed on waves of speculation and went bust with economic collapse. And always, officials from the other Washington stepped in with charters, commissions, and cash. "The country was full of robust individuals straining every effort to find places for themselves on the public payroll," quipped Washington state historian Murray Morgan. Across Puget Sound, rail lines and the Alaska gold rush spurred the frontier towns of Seattle and Tacoma into sizable cities, but the peninsula remained remote and stubbornly disconnected. Through it all, its wild heart—the mountains, rivers, and ancient forests—persevered remarkably intact.

For more than a century, the history of the Olympic Peninsula played out between economic forces of exploitation and nascent efforts toward conservation. From furs to timber to fish, resource industries gained solid purchase on the peninsula early on, but visions of conservation were not far over the horizon. By the early decades of the twentieth century, Americans had seen their original forests disappear: the oak woodlands of New England, the great hardwood forests of the southern Appalachians, and the virgin pine stands of the Great Lakes states. The remote Olympic Peninsula offered an opportunity to preserve some of the most outstanding primeval forests in the west, and by the 1930s, a campaign to

Clouds swirl over the twin summits of Warrior Peak and rugged basalt ridges on the edge of Olympic National Park and the Buckhorn Wilderness in Olympic National Forest.

create a national park in the Olympics reached a nation-wide audience. Decades earlier, in 1909, Theodore Roosevelt created the 610,560-acre Mount Olympus National Monument primarily to protect habitat for the declining population of Olympic elk. The opening of the Olympic Loop Highway in 1931 brought motorized tourism to the western peninsula, and for the first time visitors could easily experience the grandeur of the peninsula's forests.

National conservation organizations, scientific societies, and natural history museums took up the cause for a park, and in 1937 President Franklin Roosevelt visited the peninsula to look into the issue. He toured Lake Crescent, Lake Quinault, and the west-side forests and was favorably impressed. The following year he signed a bill creating a large national park in the Olympics with a critical provision to add more than a quarter-million acres to

TOP A Hoh Valley nurse log is covered with beadruby leaves and Oregon beaked moss. In the Olympics' temperate rain forests, down and decomposing logs provide a warm, moist seedbed for forest trees and plants. BOTTOM Roosevelt elk spend most of the year in the lowland forests of the peninsula where they browse on understory growth, seedlings, and shrubs. In the summer some elk migrate to the subalpine meadows of Olympic National Park, where they take advantage of the rich seasonal growth. OPPOSITE Bright sea lettuce adorns intertidal rocks at Sokol Point near the Chilean Memorial in Olympic National Park. Sokol Point is one of the long-term monitoring sites for measuring climate-induced changes to intertidal species over time.

protect lower rain forest valleys and a strip of land along the wild Olympic coast.

Other conservation measures had protected important parts of the peninsula's biodiversity. Olympic National Forest was designated in 1907. National wildlife refuges were established to protect important bird nesting and wintering areas on Pacific coastal islands and on the Strait of Juan de Fuca. Washington state consolidated the management of considerable resource lands, some as protected areas, and state and county parks and recreation areas began to appear. But the creation of Olympic National Park was a visionary act for its time and a groundbreaking step in sustaining the vast and interwoven network of interdependent life on the peninsula, the Olympic ecosystem. For the first

Moraine Lake occupies the former site of Anderson Glacier. The Anderson is one of a number of Olympic glaciers that have disappeared in recent decades due to climate change.

time in our country's history, large areas of forested watersheds of significant economic value were preserved in perpetuity. Unlike earlier national parks, which focused primarily on scenic high country, Olympic National Park protected year-round habitats for elk and other wildlife along with thousands of miles of pristine salmon streams. These, along with an extensive Pacific coastal area that included intertidal communities, nesting areas, and feeding grounds for fish and a host of sea mammals, make Olympic one of the most ecologically diverse parks in the nation.

The international scientific community has twice recognized the planetary importance of Olympic National Park by designating it a UNESCO Biosphere Reserve and World Heritage Site. These recognitions are echoed by more than three million visitors annually who come to the park and the peninsula to recreate year-round. The park and its surrounding wilderness areas, forests, rivers, lakes, shorelines, trails, and recreation sites represent one of the most diverse and spectacular natural areas on the planet.

Through the ages, the Olympic ecosystem has proven remarkably resilient. However, the shifting climate and geographic isolation that fostered such outstanding biodiversity in the Olympics now pose threats to the long-term health of the ecosystem. As the pace of human-caused global warming accelerates, glaciers disappear and mountain snowpacks dwindle. Subalpine lakes and meadows, wetlands, wild salmon stocks, and intertidal communities are at risk. Meanwhile, the human population continues to grow. More than eight million people now live within five hours of the Olympic Peninsula. The wild and beautiful sanctuary of the Olympics is showing signs of strain. Fortunately, the past few decades have marked a sea change in our treatment of natural resources across the peninsula. The last century saw conservation make inroads into unsustainable resource use; the promise of the current century is a shift toward ecological restoration, repairing the damage incurred by decades of taking. Our task now is to meet the threat of global warming with bold visionary measures and restore degraded ecosystems.

The times have shifted profoundly in the half century since my first passage on the *Hyak*. The peninsula's storied mountains, rivers, and wilderness coast offered all the discovery and adventure I dreamed of, and a great deal more. As I've come to learn more about my adopted home, my appreciation and sense of responsibility for its future have deepened. What follows are stories I've gleaned along the way, brief views into the peninsula's past, and glimpses of a possible future. ❖

# The Quietest Spot

The Hoh Rain Forest is a muffled realm, padded as a recording studio with moss and trees and leaves. Every surface is soft and plush. A cushion of rot softens downed logs. It is a pillow palace, a place quilted with quiet in a remote corner of the lower 48.

One reason for this rare quiet is that Olympic National Park is tucked in a corner of the nation's farthest northwestern tip. No roads cross this park. There is no helicopter tourism, no funicular, no razzmatazz concession for entertainment. People don't come here for zip lines or ATV trails. Instead, the park is a place to revel in raw wilderness. And it is a place with quiet and natural soundscapes rare in this world.

To protect it, on Earth Day in 2005 Gordon Hempton of Seattle placed a small red rock 3.2 miles from the visitor's center above Mount Tom Creek Meadows on the Hoh River Trail, about a two-hour hike from the parking lot on a gentle path with old-growth forest, ferns, and birdsong for company. He set down the stone and declared it "One Square Inch of Silence." The idea was to defend the natural soundscape of the Olympic backcountry wilderness from the intrusion of noise made by humans. For declaring one square inch of quiet, of course, depends on preserving quiet over many square miles.

Noise is an insidious pollutant. Noise intrusions, as Hempton calls the sound of, say, an airplane, can't be screened out like an unpleasant view. A professional sound recordist, Hempton has roamed the world recording the sounds of nature for his work—or trying to. Over the years, he has noticed places where he once could reliably record natural sounds have been spoiled by noise intrusion. In one place after another, the sound of rain, the hiss of summer grass, or the buzz of a bee became so frequently invaded by human-made noise that he could no longer record the natural sound of the place.

Even his beloved Olympic National Park is under siege. When Hempton first began his campaign for quiet, he was largely concerned about the noise of commercial aircraft. Then came the US Navy, with the roar of Growler jets in training maneuvers right over the park. Even the low rumble of the jets at an idle rattles water in a glass miles away. A peer-reviewed study of the Growlers' noise impact has revealed that orcas are exposed to their noise at a depth of more than one hundred feet underwater. Scientists have found the noise levels generated by the jets at times are high enough to damage human hearing.

Since Hempton founded the One Square Inch of Silence Foundation (onesquareinch.org) to defend quiet at Olympic National Park, the cause has grown to celebrate and protect the sounds of nature from noise pollution around the world through the all-volunteer Quiet Parks International campaign. The nonprofit is dedicated to preserving natural quiet for the benefit of all life and has a simple but powerful goal: securing a world in which everyone has daily access to quiet and the opportunity to listen to the sounds of nature.

Ironically for someone whose life has revolved around listening, over the years, Hempton has suffered profound hearing loss. Yet he still talks with deep feeling and knowing about the acoustic beauty of Olympic National Park. Because, as Hempton likes to say, "Silence is not the absence of something, but the presence of everything."

In Hempton's view, Olympic National Park is an amphitheater for some of the most beautiful sounds on Earth: the bugle of an elk on an autumn night, the song of a Swainson's thrush in June, the rake of the tide through stones in a winter storm at Rialto Beach.

When he is in the park, he likes to focus on the farthest away sound he can hear—and then extend his listening horizon even farther. "Simply listen to the whole place, as you would at a performance hall," Hempton said. "Every season has its music. There is not a good or a bad time to go. Just go."

—Lynda V. Mapes

**Along Tshletshy Creek in the Queets Valley in Olympic National Park, a quiet alder bottom receives a jolt of early-summer sunlight. Protecting natural sounds and quiet is a priority for conservation organizations, including the National Parks Conservation Association.**

# A Wild, Broken Confusion

Sunrise Ridge is a gently sloping, flower-studded arm of Hurricane Ridge. For most visitors to Olympic National Park, it's a stunning threshold to the interior mountains. As travelers round Sunrise Ridge on the final curve of the seventeen-mile Hurricane Ridge Road, the full, dazzling expanse of the snowcapped Olympic Mountains sweeps into view. Tier upon tier of etched peaks and converging ridges extend to the far horizon like the stilled waves of a tumultuous sea. Even more than my initial glimpse of the Olympics from the deck of the *Hyak*, the view rounding Sunrise Ridge for the first time bowled me over. I've yet to regain my balance.

From the nearby visitor center terrace I shielded my eyes as the glacier-clad summit of Mount Olympus, another seventeen miles distant, gleamed in splintered sunlight. The rugged 7,000-foot peaks of the Bailey Range stretched south around Mount Olympus like a wall around a castle fortress. Below them the deep green of the Elwha Valley held a daub of morning fog as it wended its way into the interior mountains. Snow-streaked summits of Mount Anderson and Chimney Peak floated to the south; Mount Seattle and Mount Queets anchored the far end of the Baileys. I flattened my map against the terrace wall in the light wind, but even with it, the vast tangled array of peaks and valleys was a bit disorienting. I later discovered I was not alone. Lieutenant Joseph O'Neil took in the same view after thrashing his way overland from Port Angeles in 1885. O'Neil was among the first Euro-Americans to explore the Olympics, and he kept meticulous notes. He

recorded the view from nearby Klahhane Ridge: "Looking east, west, and south, mountains, free from timber, some covered with snow, rise in wild, broken confusion."

The Olympics are young mountains composed of relatively young rocks. Geologically complex and rising abruptly from the more subdued coast ranges to the south, they are an enigma. No clear watershed divide defines the range; rather, it is a jumbled pile of peaks threaded with creeks and incised by river valleys that whirl outward in all directions. The mountains seem to revel in their own wild confusion. To me, that has always been part of their allure.

Ushered into existence by the spreading ocean floor, the Olympics return the favor by intercepting up to twenty feet of precipitation each year and sending it back to the sea by way of clean, freshwater rivers. Such rivers, or a single large river back in Tertiary time some sixty million years ago, laid the foundation of the Olympic Peninsula in what was then a shallow coastal sea. Draining a large corner of the old North American continent, ancestral rivers deposited strata of sandstones, siltstones, mudstones, and conglomerates on the seafloor. Over millions of years, these sedimentary rocks deepened, sometimes miles deep, and extended hundreds of miles out. At the same time the ocean floor itself was in motion, pushing relentlessly eastward against the continent's edge. There, the ocean-bottom plate folded beneath the continent to

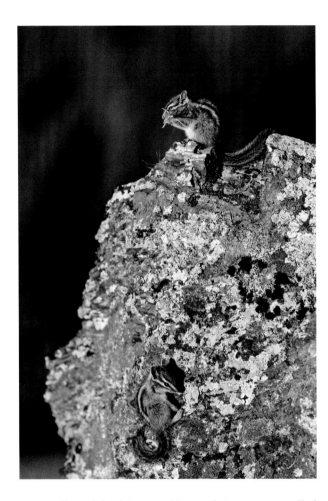

it into the large embayment formed by Vancouver Island and the old North American coast. As freight-loads of sedimentary rocks on the ocean side of the basalts continued to raft in, they were scraped off as if by a gigantic snowplow and plastered onto the continent. Once-horizontal sedimentary layers were bent, folded, broken, shuffled, and restacked willy-nilly against the upended basalts. Sometime around seventeen million years ago, the chaotic mass of rocks rose above the ocean's surface and the Olympic Mountains were born. Today, tough basalts partially encircle the range on the north, east, and south. They form Mount Storm King, Mount Angeles, Tyler Peak, and the rugged eastern peaks I first saw from the *Hyak*. Sedimentary sea-bottom rocks make up the core of the Olympic range, including the massive sandstone formations of Mount Olympus, Mount Anderson, and much of the Bailey Range.

It is a jumbled assemblage to be sure, and it caused no end of grief for twentieth-century geologists, particularly before plate tectonics theory opened the field. But it was all the same to the Pacific. Ocean-born rain and snow continued to arrive on prevailing westerly winds. Rivulets streamed off the mountain mass, formed creeks and rivers, and immediately began eroding the rocks, even as they rose to capture more rain and snow. The greater the uplift, the cooler the air, and the more moisture the mountains pulled down. The final shaping of the Olympic Peninsula, and the key to its extraordinary biological diversity, was yet to come.

An Olympic chipmunk ventured up onto the terrace wall in search of a handout. I resisted, of course, but reflected that this panhandler's distant ancestors had surely seen leaner times. About two million years ago, the earth took a decided tilt toward winter. Continental ice sheets formed and advanced into temperate regions. In western North America, the Cordilleran ice sheet pushed south from central Alaska into the area of Washington state. Massive—up to a mile thick—it collided with the Olympic Mountains on several occasions. During the most recent advance around sixteen thousand years ago, the train of ice split against the wedge of the Olympics. One lobe ground south,

eventually melt back into earth's mantle in a process called subduction. If that were the end of the story, this part of the Northwest coast would be a far less dramatic landscape. But in the area that was to become the Olympics, something else happened.

The subduction process jammed. Pressures from the colliding seafloor and the westward-drifting continent caused the continental margin to tear. This allowed the earth's mantle to upwell and cool into a submarine range of basalt seamounts. The ocean plate continued to collide with the continent, but there was no way the mass of submarine basalt and sedimentary rock was going to be swallowed by subduction. Instead the ongoing collision of plates upended the range of seamounts and crammed

LEFT **Olympic chipmunks (Tamias amoenus caurinus) are an endemic subspecies that survived the Pleistocene Ice Age in the refuge of the Olympic Mountains. They are seen here on a lichen-stippled boulder on Blue Mountain in Olympic National Park.** OPPOSITE **Smooth Douglasia is one of the many mat-forming plants that bring stony alpine environments to life. Mat- and cushion-forming plants are well adapted to harsh alpine conditions.**

carving Puget Sound; the other ploughed west, deepening the trough of the Strait of Juan de Fuca. Higher up, alpine glaciers honed and sharpened Olympic ridges and peaks and sculpted the lovely, lake-studded cirques of Royal and Seven Lakes Basins. Mountain glaciers descended into river corridors, creating broad U-shaped valleys, especially in the more heavily glaciated western Olympics.

During those times of maximum ice, the Olympic Mountains became a biological island. A thousand miles of glacier ice lay to the north and east, a vast ocean to the west, and a supercharged meltwater river formed a barrier to the south. All the while, plants and animals persisted in snow-free refuges in the isolated Olympics. Some, such as the Olympic marmot, evolved into a distinct species. Other small mountain mammals, such as my visitor the Olympic chipmunk, the Olympic snow mole, and the Mazama pocket gopher, became separate subspecies. And eleven mountain plants, including the exquisite Flett's violet and Piper's bellflower, evolved into their own species as well. These and some two dozen other Olympic endemics sailed the ark of the Olympic Mountains into our time. They are tenacious witnesses to the flux and dramatic change of climate and geography—and eloquent testaments to the sustaining power and evolutionary promise of this dynamic landscape.

When winter storms ebb and the first spring winds come to the mountains, ridge tops blow free of snow to reveal some of the hardiest alpine plants. Blue clustered spires of endemic Olympic Mountain synthyris appear

Wildflowers of Olympic National Park:
LEFT **Beargrass** BOTTOM RIGHT **Avalanche lilies** BOTTOM LEFT **Stonecrop** OPPOSITE TOP LEFT **Columbia lily** OPPOSITE RIGHT **Magenta paintbrush** OPPOSITE BOTTOM LEFT **Sitka columbine**

in March some years. South-facing meadows follow, and by May and June, avalanche lilies melt their way through the edges of snowbanks, and yellow glacier lilies follow in the wake of receding snows. Grasses and sedges regreen meadowlands. Horned larks and American pipits return to nest in open alplands, and sooty grouse take shelter in stands of subalpine fir. Most noticeably, energized Olympic marmots emerge from hibernation in April and May and their sharp warning whistles ring across greening meadows. Industrious, gregarious, and playful, marmots must feed, nurse, and rear their pups; mate; and put on fat for their seven-month hibernation, all within the few short months between the snows. They feed selectively across the meadows, choosing nutrient-rich plants such as lily, paintbrush, and broadleaf lupine as plants come into flower. Researchers found that plant diversity is higher in meadows that host marmot colonies, suggesting a long coevolutionary relationship between marmots and their subalpine world.

Endemic marmots embody the Olympic high country, but a plethora of wildlife animates summer meadows and mountain forests as winter snows winnow. Snowshoe hares thrive year-round in the Olympic high country,

venturing out nocturnally into meadows and feeding on the needles, twigs, and bark of subalpine fir and other mountain trees during winter. Columbian black-tailed deer climb to the high meadows in summer, drawn by the abundance of plants. Fawns are born in early summer, grow quickly, and in fall follow their mothers downslope to winter in lowland valleys. Chipmunks and voles grow plump on meadow growth, bending tall grass stalks down for seeds. And hawks circle the late-summer skies for unwary prey.

As berries ripen in late summer and fall, activity increases in the high country. Flocks of birds join hikers in huckleberry patches, but black bears rule the day. Like ravens, black bears are ubiquitous in the Olympics, taking advantage of productive habitats from coastal tide pools to alpine slopes. Bears venture to the high meadows in early summer and sup on the sapwood of subalpine trees when early meadow growth is insufficient. Otherwise plants, carrion, seeds, and grubs carry them over to berry season. Then a black bear can seriously stack on the pounds, gaining up to a third of its body weight before its winter rest. By mid to late October, black bears are shiny, fat, shaggy, and gorgeous. Wearing the bounty of the Olympics as a winter coat, they return

ABOVE **A curious black bear peers beneath a log into a natural hiding place for fish on the Hoh River in Olympic National Park.** OPPOSITE **A hiker traverses a subalpine meadow with Mount Duckabush on the skyline.**

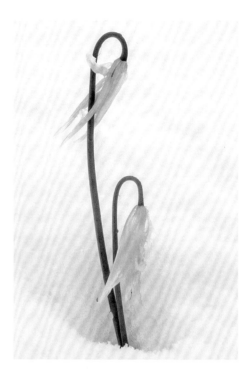

ABOVE **Flett's violet, a rare Olympic endemic, and saxifrage flowers** FAR RIGHT **Piper's bellflowers, an endemic plant of the Olympic Mountains, bloom in a rock cleft.** RIGHT **Calypso or fairy slipper orchid is one of the most delicate and beautiful forest wildflowers in the Olympics. Like many orchids, Calypso has mycorrhizal or fungus-root, connections to other forest plants.**

OPPOSITE FAR LEFT **Magenta paintbrush and lupine blossoms** OPPOSITE TOP RIGHT **A glacier lily melts through the snowpack.** OPPOSITE BOTTOM RIGHT **Yellow wood violets**

to lowland forests (by way of salmon streams) for the season's torpor. Cubs are born in the den in January and bears emerge in April, hungry for grubs and winter-killed elk and deer as the first south-facing meadows emerge from snow, and the mountain season unfolds once more.

I RETURN TO HURRICANE RIDGE ON A JULY AFTERnoon to visit with Janis Burger. Janis is an interpretive ranger and accomplished naturalist who has led thousands of walks and snowshoe hikes in the high Olympics. After nearly four decades at Olympic National Park, this is her last summer before retiring. Like me, she vividly recalls her first view of the Olympics as she rounded the curve at Sunrise Ridge back in 1982 (she was equally awestruck). I hope to get insights gleaned from a lifetime spent sharing the wonders of the Olympic Mountains with visitors.

Light, broken clouds cast shadows over the mountains, but the midsummer meadows are alight with wildflowers. We walk the popular Cirque Rim trail above the visitor center as it winds through a mosaic of subalpine fir and meadow. Soon, Janis stops to chat with an older couple about birds and then with a young family excited about their wildlife sightings: chipmunks, coyote, and a buck with antlers still in velvet. For Janis, teaching seems to come as naturally as walking, and I notice she asks more questions as she answers to draw visitors out. She tells me that the majority are from the Pacific Northwest and what they value most is the opportunity to drive a scenic paved road into the heart of mountain country. The growing numbers of international visitors are most impressed by the vast amount of public land that extends before them. The park encompasses 922,650 acres, more than 95 percent of it designated as wilderness. Olympic National Forest encompasses another 643,419 acres with some 88,000 in wilderness. "They don't have that at home," she reminds me. "It's fun to share the luxury of such a large protected wilderness."

When we reach the ridge top, the northern slope drops away into meadow, forest, and snowfields, and the ruddy cliffs of Mount Angeles dominate the skyline. "I like to engage visitors about the challenges of surviving here, the temperature variations and shallow soils, and the kinds of adaptations plants and animals have made to cope with extreme conditions." Though relatively low in elevation, the alpine and subalpine areas of the Olympics are extensive due to the range's proximity to the Pacific and abundant snow it receives. "Snow and snowmelt control everything in the subalpine," Janis observes. Plants and animals on the north sides of ridges must cope with heavy snowpacks and short growing seasons. The spirelike shapes and flexible limbs of the subalpine firs around us shed heavy snow and help insulate the trees in winter. On south slopes, drought and intense heat from the summer sun rule. Plants like broadleaf lupine grow deep taproots, while pearly everlasting sports tiny hairs that trap air, conserve moisture, and protect the plant from wind and the sun's ultraviolet rays. On ridge tops, which blow clear of snow early and are exposed to desiccating winds, plants like spreading phlox and douglasia hunker in low-growing mats and cushions and grow tough, thick leaves and stems. For Janis, part of the beauty of leading walks on the ridge is that these contrasts and adaptations are always close at hand.

What changes has she noted over her time here? Marmot colonies disappeared from parts of the ridge, Sunrise bowl and the picnic area among them. Their status is a subject of ongoing research. Then in 2014, an intrepid marmot showed up again, and others followed. In 1999, a particularly heavy snow year, some subalpine fir seedlings never emerged from the snow. Janis noticed many died as a result. In contrast, 2015 was a year of record-low snowpack. Mountain plants suffered badly and some, such as lupines, never flowered. "Of course, snowfall and snowmelt vary year by year," Janis notes, "but we're definitely in a time of declining snowpacks due to climate change." We are looping back toward the parking area now, through a flowering meadow where a marmot lopes leisurely toward its burrow. We stop, and Janis looks out over the familiar mountains, river valleys, moving clouds, and sky. "To be honest, I mostly notice how much doesn't change." ❖

Ranger-naturalist Janis Burger leads a snowshoe hike at Hurricane Ridge in Olympic National Park.

# Naming Peaks

Names can be of peculiar provenance. For example, an English trader named John Meares, bobbing on the ocean aboard the *Felice Aventureira* in the summer of 1788, spied a far-off mountain and said to himself, "If that be not the home where dwell the gods, it is certainly beautiful enough to be, and I therefore will call it Mount Olympus." Meares hadn't come that way to name things—he was there on behalf of the maritime fur trade at a time when it was exceptionally lucrative—so this sort of thing, naming a peak, was for him an ancillary pastime, or maybe a way of garnering status. At thirty-two, he already had a reputation as ungracious and deceitful, and he was sailing under a Portuguese flag for the advantages it rendered when it came to customs duties. In sum, a person of dubious repute, at sea out of pecuniary interests, applied to a mountain on a distant horizon a name he'd derived from his English education, and that name, tossed off on his quarterdeck, before long found its way into use and was subsequently pluralized into an umbrella term for over two hundred adjacent mountains. Eventually, an entire region was referred to by a variant of it, as was a national forest, a national park, and the capital of Washington state.

*Gods and Goblins: A Field Guide to Place Names of Olympic National Park* in part takes its title from the recognition that "Mount Olympus" spawned a lot of park names derived from mythology (mostly Norse, Greek, and Roman). It was a habit, in fact, among Olympic first ascenders to give peaks such names—an impulse, whether they knew it or not, that derived partly from the tangential musings of an English fur trader.

It's true that a rose by any other name smells as sweet, but it's also true that names can be usurpations, not only in the historical sense but in terms of our experience. Try as I might, I can't cross Hee Haw Creek without its name coloring my view of its waters; Petroleum Creek does a number on me, too, as do Jackass Lake and Dismal Draw. All of these names tint my thoughts and feelings, ineluctably and without much subtlety, an inflection I find everywhere, so that a rocky beach becomes "the Norwegian Memorial" for me because that's what it's called on the map I carry (a Norwegian ship broke apart there; eighteen sailors died), and Boston Swamp—just below Chicago Camp—well, they speak for themselves.

A twist: something on the order of seventy "Olympic" place names resulted from the Press Expedition, which made a one-way trip from north to south, up the Elwha and down the Quinault, in 1889 and 1890. Organized and funded by the *Seattle Press* newspaper, whose treasurer was Edmond Meany, the journey unfolded over the course of five months, during which Meany quit the *Press* and took a new job as press agent for the Washington World's Fair Association. Here we might surmise that Meany saw a useful nexus between his former job, his current one, and certain mountains in the Olympics, because of the thirty-six peaks branded as a result of the Press Expedition, twenty-three were given the names of newspaper grandees from across the United States. Mount Childs was named for the owner of the *Philadelphia Ledger*. Mount Holmes was named for the editor of the *Boston Herald*. "Olympus" might sound absurd when considered in light of the terms I've devised, but it pales when juxtaposed against Mount Agnus, named after Felix Agnus of the Baltimore *American,* or Mount Noyes, named after Crosby Noyes of the Washington, DC, *Evening Star.*

As a follow-up to my Meany shaming, you could sit alongside No Name Creek, a tributary of the East Fork of the Quinault, or camp at No Name Lake, above the Sol Duc Valley, taking, in either locale, the implied opportunity to consider what "No Name" does to you. You'll soon find it intervenes in your experience with as much force as "Hee Haw Creek" or "Lake Aldwell." Maybe I'm just promoting here the state of mind aspired to by certain haiku writers, one characterized by a focus on pure awareness without interpretation or commentary (*sick of it whatever it's called sick of the names/I dedicate every pore to what's here,* wrote Ikkyū). This stripped-down state of mind is impossible to achieve, of course, but the attempt can be rewarding. For me, the Olympics have been conducive to such efforts, not just because they're remote and mostly quiet, but because my intimacy with them deepens the challenge. They force me to look at my romanticizing of forests, my attachments to peaks, and the names I myself give to everything.

—David Guterson

The interior Olympic Mountains were the last region in Washington to be explored and mapped by Europeans, but they were frequented by Native people of the peninsula for millennia.

**Snowshoeing at Hurricane Ridge**

A winter scene of the snowclad Olympics and subalpine firs from Hurricane Hill

## Marmot Monitoring

EEE comes the marmot's shriek, announcing the presence of marmots in their grassy mountain meadow redoubt—and their alertness to yours.

One of the delights of the high country, marmots live throughout the Olympic Mountains above four thousand feet. Most of their habitat is protected within Olympic National Park. Social and gregarious, *Marmota olympus* spend their summer days nuzzling, playing, and chirping. Long summer days are for haying and flower-picking in the same mountain meadows hikers enjoy. Relatives of the prairie dog, marmots live in burrows in colonies with other families in their cohort. Pups are born in their burrow. Marmots weigh up to about fifteen pounds and rival pikas for their sweet face, which is married to a woodchuck's rotund and fuzzy body.

Because they have no sweat glands, a common summer sight is a marmot lying flat as a rug on a rock, bare dirt, or snow patch to cool down. Olympic marmots dine on fresh, tender flowering plants such as lupine and glacier lilies, but earlier in the year marmots may subsist on roots and can even be found gnawing on trees. During the summer, marmots really pack it on, doubling their body weight so they can live off their stored fat during their long winter's nap of seven to eight months.

The local population of marmots in the Olympics is endemic, meaning this type of marmot lives nowhere else. While they've been noted in the meadows of the Olympics since the 1880s, park researchers detected a decline in marmot populations of about 7 percent per year from 2002 to 2006. The cause was determined to be coyote predation, particularly on pregnant females. That sparked the creation of the Olympic National Park Marmot Monitoring Program, launched by the National Park Service in 2010 to get citizen science volunteers out in the park to survey the mammals' habitat regularly.

"Here is a species that is visible and occurs in a place where people like to hike. I thought, we can design a citizen science program that will give us meaningful data," said Patti Happe, wildlife branch chief at Olympic National Park. She helped create and launch the program, which is funded entirely by donations from Washington's National Park Fund. "The group of volunteers who come out to do this—it is essential. We would not be doing it without them; we just could not sustain this program," Happe said.

Not a marmot count per se, the surveys are used to understand how much of the marmots' suitable habitat is being utilized. In 2022 Happe had 122 volunteers planning to spend from three to eight days in the field, searching in groups of two to six for the presence of marmots in their known habitat. "We could never hire enough field crews to do that," Happe said. Sixty percent of the volunteers are returning for another round of monitoring. "I don't really recruit anymore," Happe said. "They recruit their friends." By now some thirty-five thousand volunteer hours have been logged.

Volunteers are given a day of training and practice in the field to learn how to use their GPS data logger and data sheets. They learn how to spot not only the animals themselves but also marmot burrows, as well as how to tell if the burrow is occupied or abandoned. The park provides all the permits, but volunteers need to bring their gear and find their own way around.

So what are these citizen scientists learning?

So far volunteers have detected that the declines of the 2000s have not continued, and the marmots' rate of occupancy of their habitat has stabilized. But it is low, at about 50 percent, Happe said. That makes long-term monitoring all the more important to help guide decisions in the future about the Olympic marmot.

If, for instance, marmot habitat becomes unsuitable due to climate change, that will spark an ethical question about whether to alter the landscape, such as by cutting trees to reopen alpine meadows, to suit an already altered environment, Happe said. While she doesn't know what the future holds, Happe knows long-term data will be essential to decision-making. "I feel it is really critically important we monitor this species; it is found nowhere else in the world," Happe said. "It is our unique responsibility."

—Lynda V. Mapes

ABOVE **A marmot family keeps watch at a burrow entrance.** OPPOSITE **A young marmot cuddles an adult.**

**Sunlight penetrates rugged Glines Canyon below the old Glines Canyon Dam on the Elwha River in Olympic National Park.**

# Klallaṃ Mountains
# nəxʷsƛ̓áyəm̓sx̣əykʷəy̓é?č

*Jamie R. Valadez, Lower Elwha Klallam Tribe*

## Čáy̓əqʷ

Our ancestors made sure they passed down the history and traditional knowledge of the Klallam Mountains. It was their hope and dream that someday their descendants would once again return to the backwoods. As Elwha River restoration was ramping up, tribal programs were being established to reintroduce the Klallam people to the mountains where our Ancestors fished, hunted, and gathered:

- A group of tribal youth from the Lower Elwha Klallam Tribe hiked the Low Divide from the Elwha River to Quinault in 2002. That was the year Quinault was hosting the annual Canoe Journeys. Along the way, the youth renamed ancient seasonal camps in Klallam, and so sčiʔanəŋáwtxʷ (Place of Our Ancestors) became the name for Lillian River; sməyəcáwtxʷ (Place of the Elk) became the name for Elkhorn; sx̣əykʷəy̓é?č spə́ɫxən (Place of the Mountain Meadow) became the name for Hayes; čə́q sqiqəyáyŋəxʷ (Place of the Big Trees) became the name for Chicago Camp; and ʔəsq̓apɫáwtxʷ (Gathering Place) became the name of Low Divide.
- Every summer since 2005, a camp has been held for our youth at NatureBridge, a natural science center located on Lake Crescent. The youth learn about the Elwha River restoration as well as traditional knowledge about the mountains by hiking the trails to sacred places and seasonal camps.
- The Creation Site was found in 2012 as Lake Aldwell was drained. Tribal members began to revive the tradition of hiking to the Creation Site as part of their vision quest experience.

- Since the restoration, it has been difficult to hike along the Elwha River, so groups began to hike to other places in the mountains such as Obstruction Point and both Olympic Hot Springs and Sol Duc Hot Springs.
- Quinault hosted Canoe Journeys again in 2013, when another group of youth experienced the hike from Elwha to Quinault.
- In 2014 a group hiked the Seven Lakes Basin Loop, and some of the hikers went on to hike to Boston Charlie's Camp.

Along with the successful restoration of the Elwha River, the Klallam people have also restored their relationship with the Klallam Mountains. Along the way, they learned about their Ancestors and the teachings and traditional knowledge that they passed down about the Olympic Mountains. What follows is some of this oral history.

## Creation Site

The Klallam people were created on the Elwha River at a place where a rock formation is shaped like a coil basket, called spčúʔ. Our very beginning came from this coiled basket, shaped within the rock, where dirt was scooped and out of which the human race was formed. All of the tribes of this region were created at this sacred place on the Elwha River. This is where the Creator, known as x̣áyəs, bathed the first people and blessed them. This is now where our people go on their vision quests. If a man thrusts his hand into the water there and brings out deer hair, for example, he knows he will be a good hunter.

An elk calf nurses from its mother.

## Vision Quest

Every day the Klallam people bathed in the Elwha River, but when they went on their vision quests, they went to the Olympic Hot Springs or Sol Duc Hot Springs to purify themselves and receive spiritual guidance.

Spirit power came from living things, natural objects, natural forces, monsters, and even handmade objects on rare occasions. Training for going on a vision quest began when children were small; they would be instructed to bathe and scrub in icy water and to go out on dark and stormy nights. As the children neared puberty, they began fasting. When an individual was "clean," the spirit power would come to them. The spirit gave a song to its new owner that brought their power into force—the song itself was a spiritual or physical entity.

When a person returned from a spirit quest, that individual kept the event quiet for a year until the spirit was revealed at the next potlatch and their spirit song was sung. Guardian spirits visited their owners once a year. When the power came, the person became ill. Instead of calling a shaman in, the Klallam called in friends to help sing their spirit songs for several days, until the spirit was satisfied and left. The only difference between a shaman's power and that of a layperson was the way in which power was acquired. The spirit power provided a form of wealth that would bring prestige to the individual. Although spirit acquisition was a personal achievement, the benefits were often shared by the village. The halibut spirit, for example, could make fish come to the shore so that all of the village could acquire them. The thunderbird spirit was the strongest spirit, and the most difficult to obtain. A warrior with this spirit power for war could shoot lightning into another person.

## Sacred Places

In the upper Elwha, there is a place called the Meadows. This is a special healing place where Klallams would go gather medicinal plants.

Joe and Emily Sampson lived on the Hunter John Homestead on the Elwha River. When their son Charlie was a young boy, he started to get sick. This was during a time when the whole village was being ravaged by disease, and many people were dying. There was no cure. So Joe and Emily decided to take Charlie and go live in isolation upriver at the Meadows, located by Lake Mills on the eastern slope. They lived there for eight years in isolation. The people who lived down below could see the smoke coming up from the Meadows, so they knew that the Sampsons still lived. After eight years they moved back down to the homestead. Charlie returned as a healthy young man.

A Klallam man named Boston Charlie used to hunt elk in the mountains. He was born in 1828 and he died in 1928. He spent his summers in the mountains and had a favorite spot that he camped at every year. Today it's called Boston Charlie's Camp and is located at the base of Cat Peak. Boston Charlie was the last medicine man of the Klallam people. He would go up to the hot springs to fast, pray, and cleanse himself every year. The last time he traveled into the mountains, he had a very close call: he must have fallen and hurt himself, for he was immobile, weak, and didn't have anything to eat for several days. He later told how the sun was going down and a huge being came up from a cliff. He thought to himself, "Now, this is the day I am going to die." The being held great big leaves carrying blueberries and thimbleberries, and it was wet. He put the moist berries in Boston Charlie's mouth and then disappeared down the cliff. Boston Charlie survived his ordeal with a bigfoot, called číčəyíqʷtən, and that was the last time he went up into the mountains.

## The Flood Story

**Joe Sampson told this story in 1925:** "There was a man who told his people to make some canoes and to make them large and strong so they could endure storms. There was a flood coming. The people said the mountains were high and they could just go up the mountains when the flood came. He warned them again. Soon it began to rain and rained for many days. And the rivers became salt. The people said they would go up the mountains. . . . They had no way of getting to the mountains, for the valleys were full of water and the rivers overflowed their banks.

The people that walked all died. Those that had canoes and water and food lived. Some who were in a canoe tied themselves to a treetop then their canoe hit the trees and split. Many died. Some tied themselves to mountains, and the highest ones were saved. One of the mountains that saved the Klallam has been described by many people and appears to be either Mount Carrie or Mount Olympus."

## Thunderbird

**Ed Sampson told the following story about the thunderbird:** "There is a bathing spot about where the lower dam is. The thunderbird lives on the hill above the rock cliffs. You can see him sitting up there like an eagle. The Indians would bathe there and not eat anything. They just starve themselves while they're bathing. Then when they think they are clean enough, they try to reach the thunderbird. When they get part way up, if that thunderbird doesn't think the person is clean enough, it starts shooting its lightning at him, and he must retreat. There was only one man who made it. He stayed there a week preparing himself. When he got up there, there was a big white rock. He went around it and saw a hole on the other side. That was the thunderbird's door. He got a stick and put it across the hole. He knew that if he didn't, once he got inside, that hole would seal up and he would be locked in. When he went in, he saw an old man with white hair and white whiskers sitting way up like a king. That was the thunderbird himself. Everything inside was gold and diamonds. Thunderbird had his hunting and fishing gear up on the side of the room. The thunderbird asked him what he wanted; the Indian told him he wanted a spirit so he could catch fish easily, and he picked out a fishhook, cəmúʔəs, for catching halibut that was made out of gold. The thunderbird reached out and grabbed that fishhook and threw it at the Indian. The Indian crawled back through the hole and took the stick and threw it away. When the thunderbird goes out fishing it is so powerful, they can see it flying back hanging onto a big whale. Just like an eagle with a fish in its mouth."

## Lightning

Our grandparents were fishing. They came ashore and were sitting next to their fire watching the lightning out in the straits. One bolt of lightning landed on the water, way out there, and pretty soon it started swimming toward shore. It showed itself, just like a big beast or monster. Like an alligator or crocodile. It came right ashore, not far from where they landed, and started walking straight up the bank, over a hundred feet up. When it got on top, it went after a big cedar tree and started climbing that. When it got up there, that lightning took off again and the tree started burning.

## Klallam Warriors Had Thunderbird Spirit Power

When another tribe kills someone from here, just as soon as the word comes that someone was murdered, they get their weapons ready and shove out in their canoes. As soon as they do, the skies get dark with clouds and it begins to thunder and lightning. The last place where thunder was near the water was the first hill from the Elwha, but now thunder is way up in the mountains near the warm springs. If you get close you will see sparks. Thunder and lightning were a warning to other tribes that the Klallam warriors were coming.

A storm had arisen, and the thunderbird at this juncture began to flap his wings and open and shut his eyes in the heavens, and the lightning snake sailed forth from beneath that warring bird's breast . . . and quicker than it takes the thunderbird to flap his wings, hundreds of painted warriors fell to earth and the Klallam Indians then held the land.

The Elwha River was home to the thunderbird, who lived in a cave and chased the salmon upriver by sending thunder and lightning towards the mouth of the river. When the lightning hit the water it turned into a two-headed serpent. When the thunderbird did this, the Klallam people prepared to fish because they knew a good run of fish was coming. The thunderbird helped the people in this way.

**A murmuration of snowy plover and dunlin graces the sky in front of the Dungeness Bay Lighthouse.**

## Elwha River Seasonal Fishing Camp
### ʔéʔɬxʷaʔ stúʔwiʔ caʔɬaʔŋéʔiɬ

There were at least thirteen seasonal camps and two permanent villages up the Elwha River. One of the villages was titiʔəɬ, Klallam Village, located where Indian Creek empties into the Elwha. The other was located where Little River empties into the Elwha. The people who lived at Indian Creek were considered hunters, and the name of the headman of this village was Hunter John. This village was flooded by the Elwha Dam construction. A few families were still living at this village, and many others were utilizing it seasonally.

The Elwha Klallam hunted for elk, deer, and other land game and birds in the backcountry prairies and mountain meadows. They also practiced vision questing, bathing in both the Olympic Hot Springs and Sol Duc Hot Springs. They gathered plants used for food, medicine, or making baskets. They traveled by canoe up the river and hiked trails to go up into the high country. They met Skokomish, Quinault, and other tribes in the backcountry. There were trails where the Elwha River meets the Hoh River, the Quileute River, and the Quinault River. Descendants of Hunter John have recollections of camping locations in the mountainous regions of the Elwha. Happy Lake was an established campsite until the 1930s. Another was located on Hurricane Hill ridge, at Windfall Creek.

There was a trail that led to the foot of a mountain spur called Devil's Backbone. This trail traversed a steep mountainside and descended to the river bottom where there was an old Indian smokehouse, probably across from Boulder Creek. Boulder Creek was a hunting camp where Boston Charlie gaffed large Chinook salmon and where the Indians kept canoes. Farther upriver, at Idaho Creek, there was an old wringing post used for dressing

BELOW **The late-season flow of the Elwha River spills past autumn foliage. The now free-flowing Elwha is the site of the largest salmon restoration project in the United States.** OPPOSITE **A male black-tailed deer browsing in the Elwha Valley**

elk hides. The Klallam hunted elk in the mountains as far as Elwha Lake, past the mountains. (Elwha Lake could be a lake dammed by a landslide up the Elwha or a high alpine lake.) Boston Charlie hunted elk up as far as the headwaters of the Elwha. They also hunted elk east and west of Mount Olympus.

Joe Sampson made trips to the Hayes River, where he saw large Chinook salmon, and the area around Boulder Creek was a Klallam camp where large Chinook were gaffed. Ed Sampson recalled, "In March to May, there were king salmon, about forty-five to fifty pounds. From May to August, there were coho, about thirty-five to forty pounds. From October to November, there were chum, about fifty pounds. From November to December, every fourth year, there were humpies, about fifteen to twenty pounds. There were steelhead from October to November. The fish were very bright near the mouth of the river and gradually darkened upstream."

Henry Charles described fishing at a weir in 1952: "The weir consists of a series of bipods set into the stream with a pole laid across them. Against this go sections of woven lattice work. There is a platform where the fisherman lies with his head against the signal stick. He brings the fish up with a gaff hook or spear or dip net. My father fished at a weir on the Elwha River. He slept there night and day."

The importance of salmon is evidenced by its prominence in ritual and by the care required in its handling. The first salmon of the season is boiled into a soup, and the entire village partakes in the meal. Each village may have had a ritual revolving around a different species of salmon, unique to a particular river drainage. One thing common to all the tribes is that the salmon was revered so that it would return to its abode the next season.

These are some of the sacred places along the Elwha River and the Olympic Mountains that the Klallams utilized for fishing, hunting, and gathering. It has been ten years now since the two dams have been removed from the Elwha River. Restoration is happening as nature brings balance back to this beautiful land. The Klallam people also have returned and are practicing their traditions as our elders had hoped would happen.

An old-growth Douglas-fir–western hemlock forest in Olympic National Park's Sol Duc Valley. Old growth can take centuries to develop and harbors a rich diversity of habitats for a range of wildlife.

# The High Society of Trees

During my early years on the Olympic Peninsula, I earned a living by planting trees on cutover forest lands. For part of each winter and spring my crew and I loaded our trucks, trailers, and campers and caravanned into the rain-washed foothills. We moved our camps from job to job like nomads. The work was vigorous, but our camps were splendid, tucked into riverside trees or perched high on logging landings overlooking the Pacific or the Strait of Juan de Fuca. We dried soaked boots and warmed tired bones by airtight wood stoves. Redolent with smoke and rain, we counted ourselves among the lucky few. Tree planting took me to remote corners of the peninsula and gave me a wider and deeper sense of the land. Olympic National Park and the roadless areas of Olympic National Forest dominate over a million acres at the heart of the peninsula, but twice that amount of land makes up the "working forest" that surrounds it. Managed by the US Forest Service, the Washington Department of Natural Resources, timber companies, tribes, and private landowners, most of it was available for logging—and logged it was. By the mid-1970s, close to two billion board feet of timber was coming off the Olympic Peninsula each year, and work for our small reforestation company was plentiful. Tree planting gave me and my fellow planters an opportunity to put something back into the forestry equation. I recall standing on landings at the end of countless jobs and looking out over steep clearcut slopes. The bright green of thousands of newly planted seedlings radiated a sense of hope.

The forests of the Olympic Peninsula are legendary. For millennia, they supplied the broad, split-cedar planks of longhouses that characterized Native villages, perhaps a hundred or more along the peninsula's coasts. Thick trunks of western redcedar were shaped elegantly into long seagoing canoes. Red cedar was the basis of material culture for Northwest Coast people. Clothing, baskets, boxes, cooking utensils, mats, masks, and spear shafts: all early gifts from the trees.

And the forests were vast. In 1792, Archibald Menzies, sailing with Captain George Vancouver, described the forests along the Strait of Juan de Fuca as "luxurious,"

extending "as far as the eye can reach." A half century later, American explorer Charles Wilkes found the peninsula's shores "covered with a forest of various species of pines, that rises almost to the highest points of the range of mountains." Prophetically he dubbed the peninsula "a storehouse of wealth with its forests, furs, and fishes." Louis Henderson, botanist with the 1890 O'Neil expedition, saw the giant western redcedar, Douglas-fir, and Sitka spruce of the Olympics as "rivaling the famed redwoods of the Californian forests." A decade later, when Arthur Dodwell and Theodore Rixon surveyed the newly created 3,483-square-mile Olympic Forest Reserve, they stated it plainly: "Taken as a whole this is the most heavily forested region of Washington, and, with few exceptions, the most heavily forested region in the country."

There is no secret to the peninsula's remarkable wealth of trees. A superabundance of rain, a temperate coastal climate, glacier-formed valleys, and topographic diversity have given rise to some of the most biologically productive forests on earth. The sheer extravagance of growth in the peninsula's west-side rain forest valleys, estimated at 250 tons per acre, represents the greatest amount of living matter per acre in the world, far exceeding tropical forests. Consequently, the peninsula's ancient forests store more carbon than most other forests on the planet. As we hurtle headlong into global warming, this may be one of the forest's most critical functions. On dryer northern and eastern sides of the peninsula, where moisture-laden Pacific winds have been wrung dry, old-growth Douglas-fir-western hemlock forests dominate the slopes. Higher east-side stands of pine and juniper and lowland Garry oak woodlands add diversity to the Olympic ecosystem.

During short breaks from planting trees, I'd recharge my spirits on hikes in the temperate rain forest valleys of Olympic National Park. Immersing myself in the green, mossy world of undisturbed forest, even during the ever-present rains of early spring, never failed to restore me.

To visit the Olympic rain forest in spring is to enter a world burgeoning with life. Rivers run full with rain and snowmelt, and harlequin ducks come inland from the ocean to breed. The woods are alive with birdsong by day and the singing of chorus frogs at night. Trailside ferns and newly greening shrubs show recent browsing by Roosevelt elk, which are never far off. Tiered leaves of vine maples reach horizontally to catch the filtered light. Beneath them, the small, inconspicuous blooms of spring beauty and evergreen violet wink quietly among mosses. A crimson salmonberry blossom seems poised for a visit from a rufous hummingbird. And above it all massive old trees, Sitka spruce, western hemlock, and western redcedar rise like moss-flecked pillars from lush carpets of oxalis and fern. Down trees upholstered with moss bristle with tree seedlings. Every horizontal surface is crowded with growth, but the forest floor is kept surprisingly open by browsing elk. When rain eases, the full-throated voice of the river echoes through dripping trees.

The Sitka spruce-western hemlock forests that blanket the Olympics' west-side valleys are a coastal forest community that extends from southern Oregon to Alaska. Sitka spruce is a striking tree, nearly cylindrical in form with scaly purplish bark and blue-green bottlebrush needles. Rain forest spruces commonly reach diameters of eight feet and heights exceeding two hundred feet. Wind-firm and tolerant of salt spray, Sitka spruce dominates the rugged storm-washed Pacific coast but extends inland only as far as the coastal fog belt will allow. On the peninsula, the wide, glacier-carved western valleys align with prevailing coastal weather systems and funnel copious amounts of rain as well as summer fog into inland valleys. Rainfall at the Hoh Visitor Center approaches twelve feet per year. Nourished by this Noah-esque precipitation, sheltered from coastal wind storms and protected from fire and drought by summer fog—which condenses in the canopies and drips generously to the forest floor—temperate rain forests host some of the largest trees of their kind in the world.

Follow a giant spruce or hemlock from the mossy buttress of its roots and you'll become lost in an intricate network of arboreal life. The rain forest is roofed in mosses. More than 130 species of lichens, liverworts, ferns, and other epiphytes cover the limbs and trunks of rain forest trees in luxuriant aerial gardens. Selaginella clubmoss,

A rain forest nurse log supports a row of mature trees in Olympic National Park. Like most trees in the temperate rain forest, these started as seedlings on a down log. When nurse logs decompose, surviving trees sometimes form a "colonnade."

licorice fern, cat-tail moss, and others form scarves, mounds, fronds, and pillows extending sometimes hundreds of feet upwards. In early spring, before maples and alders leaf out, the canopy glows with a thousand shades of green. Drawing nutrients from the atmosphere, rain, and organic detritus, intricate, layered canopy gardens support a unique assemblage of birds, small mammals, and a host of invertebrates and microorganisms. Canopy plants fix nitrogen, distill and drip nutrients to forest plants including the trees themselves, or blow down in winter to provide an important food for deer and elk. Through these and other functions, the canopy community is central to the long-term health of the forest.

Rain forest trees may live for centuries. Six hundred years is not terribly old for a Douglas-fir; a gnarled and battered western redcedar may reach a thousand. When they die, their standing "snags" often remain to house pileated woodpeckers who carve nesting cavities; spotted owls, other birds, and a number of small mammals nest in them. Once fallen, down trees host galleries of bark beetles and wood borers. These colonizers initiate a procession of invertebrates, microbes, and fungi that recycle nutrients, carbon, and nitrogen to forest soils and provide habitat for myriad creatures along the way. Down trees offer fertile seedbeds to tree seedlings as well, giving them a leg up from the moss and plant-crowded forest floor. Most rain forest trees get their starts on such nurse logs. Colonnades of mature trees lined up along a vanished nurse log, or stilted trees whose roots embrace the ghost of a former stump or root wad, bear eloquent witness to unbroken continuity: new life perpetually springing from old.

Beneath the soil, a near-miraculous connection between fungi, forest trees, and other plants informs and unites the entire forest ecosystem. Fungi permeate the forest; their fruiting bodies, mushrooms and conks, appear everywhere. Underground, their mycelia form mycorrhizal partnerships with trees and other plants. Mycorrhizas help trees absorb up to half their water, stimulate growth, and help inhibit disease and root grazing. They provide up to 40 percent of a tree's nitrogen as well as phosphorus and other nutrients in exchange for sugars, carbon, amino acids, and other photosynthates from trees. These networks extend from treetops to root hairs and link nearly every tree in the forest, with the largest and oldest trees lending support to the smallest. Even different species exchange nutrients and information; they can communicate chemical alarm signals, suggesting the forest ecosystem could be seen as a singular organism. Mycorrhizas spread by spores, but also by small fungi-munching mammals, such as deer mice, voles, and flying squirrels, which in turn feed fishers, spotted owls, and other forest predators. Rather than an assemblage of species, the old-growth forest community is a complex and interlocking web of mutual relationships that have evolved over millions of years. Trees in ancient forests are old, but the forest itself is timeless.

One creature that has shaped the character of the temperate rain forest profoundly is its most charismatic: Roosevelt elk. Even when elk aren't seen in the rain forest, their presence looms large. Fresh tracks churn muddy bottomlands, browsed ferns and shrubs testify to recent visits, and their trails and scat are everywhere. Named for an early protector,, they were the reason Theodore Roosevelt created Mount Olympus National Monument, forerunner to the national park. Today the park protects the largest undisturbed population of Roosevelt elk in the world. Catching a glimpse of one in the rain forest or high meadows is a highlight of any visit to the peninsula.

Roosevelt elk are a coastal forest subspecies and the largest of the North American elk. They owe their stature to the incredible productivity of the rain forest combined with a mild maritime climate that limits snowfall in the valleys and allows easy winter access to food. The forest affords protection from storms, and highly nutritious winter food rains down from the canopy in the form of foliose lichens. These and other factors have combined to produce a marvelous animal. Bulls weigh up to one thousand pounds, and their thick, branched antlers may extend three feet or more in length. Elk are most easily seen in the valleys in autumn when bulls have assembled "harems" for the fall rut, and their distinctive bugling resounds throughout the forest. Most elk reside in the lower valleys year-round, but upper-valley herds migrate to high meadows in summer. Some three thousand elk reside year-round in the park; the estimated peninsula population ranges from nine thousand to twelve thousand.

To gage the influence of browsing elk herds on rain forest valleys, researchers constructed fenced exclosures on valley floors. They discovered the amazing extent elk groom the forest. Inside the exclosures, vegetation became junglelike. Salmonberry, huckleberry, and other shrubs grew thick and tall. Sword ferns reached waist-height, and vine maple and hemlock trees proliferated. In contrast, where elk grazed outside the exclosures, open, grassy glades, low herbs and forbs, and fewer trees prevailed. In fact, many of the plants that other forest herbivores prefer were much more plentiful on grazed lands. Not only do elk shape the composition of the forest floor, but evidence also suggests that by preferring hemlock seedlings over Sitka spruce, elk influence the very structure of the rain forest. Like Olympic marmots in the high meadows, elk have coevolved with their rain forest habitats. When we take in the beauty of centuries-old rain forest groves, we're witnessing the millennia-long presence of elk.

For the past century, the evolutionary processes that forged the elk-rain forest relationship has been disrupted. Elk's top predator, the wolf, was trapped and hunted from peninsula forests. The return of wolves to Yellowstone has resulted in more stable and resilient elk herds and a cascade of ecological benefits that ripple throughout the ecosystem, from songbirds to grizzlies. Cougar continue to prey on elk in the Olympics, and black bears take occasional calves, but the keystone predator that kept elk and deer populations healthy, vigorous, and in dynamic equilibrium with their forest environment is sadly missing from peninsula forests. As elk and other species cope with the effects of a warming climate, the presence of this top predator is essential. ❖

Unalaska bunchberry and horsetail are often found in the shaded woods of Olympic forests.

Fall burnishes maple, cottonwood, and alder leaves along the Elwha River.

LEFT **A pileated woodpecker tends a pair of fledglings at their nest cavity.** ABOVE **Among the more raucous members of the corvid family, Steller's jays occur at most elevations on the peninsula up to tree line.** OPPOSITE TOP LEFT **Townsend's warblers can be found year-round on the peninsula but are most often seen during breeding season along rivers and in woods.** OPPOSITE TOP RIGHT **A pair of adult osprey feed at their nest.** OPPOSITE BOTTOM RIGHT **A male rufous hummingbird is caught mid-flight.** OPPOSITE BOTTOM LEFT **Sooty grouse are found year-round on the peninsula; they frequent forests from lowlands almost up to tree line.**

# Forest Giants

The Olympic Peninsula is a land of giants, home to more champion or near-champion trees than just about anywhere else. "Big Spruce" says the sign pointing toward the eminence that presides at the end of a trail to the Quinault Giant Sitka Spruce. It's the largest in the world, estimated to be at least one thousand years old.

Such monarchs of the forest make humans feel small indeed—small in stature and brief in our lifespan on a magnificent Earth. Gifts of awe and wonder, there are few places where trees of such antiquity and size persist.

Several factors make such greatness possible. The coastal temperate climate and sweet seep of rain—twelve to fourteen feet a year—that drenches the terrain west of the Olympics provide ideal growing conditions. Large fires are rare. Several tree species native to the region, particularly western redcedar and Douglas-fir, also have the capacity to grow to truly great size and age when the conditions are just to their liking. At two hundred years, Douglas-fir is just beginning to hit its stride in a reign that can continue for centuries.

Cedar and spruce can also grow to magnificent size and venerable age. Take, for example, the Quinault Giant Sitka Spruce, measured when the American Forests Association named it the 2007 national champion at 191 feet tall and 17.7 feet in diameter, with a crown spread of 96 feet. The 1999 national champion red cedar presides over the Quinault Big Cedar Trail on the North Shore Road at 159 feet high and 761 inches around, with a 45-foot crown spread. A soaring 246-foot-high grand fir, the biggest in Olympic National Park at 229 inches around with a 43-foot crown spread, looms over the southeast side of the Duckabush Trail.

These giant trees are more than just big. Big old trees aren't just larger versions of younger trees. They have ecological properties that come only with great age. Their tops are broken and snaggle-toothed. At their bases, they are buttressed and carved with cavities and hidey-holes. Their canopies are festooned with epiphytes and mosses, habitat unto themselves. The broad branches of these venerables are home to animals from spotted owls to marbled murrelets to flying squirrels that nest, shelter, and feed preferentially in giant trees.

Big trees are the keystones of complex forest ecosystems that no young, single-age, monoculture tree farm can match. As they abide, big trees don't just stand there. Big trees grow by gobbling carbon dioxide, a greenhouse gas in the atmosphere that traps heat and warms the climate. Through the miracle of photosynthesis, atmospheric carbon is locked harmlessly away in trees both living and dead. After death, big trees are home to even more life than when they were alive, with billions of tiny microbes and decomposers that over many centuries return their nutrient riches to the soil.

In old and mature natural forests, the long cycles of time tell their stories. Broken tops of the ancients bespeak the winter storms endured. Gaps between fallen giants allow sunlight to reach the forest floor and foretell the future as a new generation rises amid an understory alive with forest herbs, shrubs, and ferns.

Step into their kingdom of green: forests of big trees invite you to take a deep breath and welcome the privilege of profound humility amid such grandeur.

—Lynda V. Mapes

**The Olympic Peninsula's abundant rainfall and mild temperate climate foster trees of exceptional size. Several record or near-record trees occur here. Part of this thousand-year-old Kalaloch cedar collapsed in a storm in 2014.**

TOP LEFT **Blue-leaf huckleberries, tastiest of all, have been enjoyed by humans in the high Olympics for millennia.** TOP RIGHT **A quiet summer camp at Hoh Oxbow on Washington Department of Natural Resources land in the lower Hoh Valley** BOTTOM RIGHT **Pacific rhododendron, Washington's state flower, is a hallmark of spring in eastern Olympic forests.** BOTTOM LEFT **Ripeness and sweetness bring a smile.** OPPOSITE **Hikers pause on a footlog bridge over the Sol Duc River in Olympic National Park.**

The decomposing wood of a western redcedar exhibits rainbow hues of molds, fungi, moss, and lichen in the lowland forest of Olympic National Park.

# Four Strong Pillars

*Loni Greninger et. al., Jamestown S'Klallam Tribe*

## shiyíɬ cə c'əx̣tánɬ.
## Our heritage and culture is our life.

The title statements in these four short essays are foundational values of the stə́tíləm nəxʷsx̣ʾáyəmˑ(Jamestown S'Klallam Tribe). To provide a mental image, each value represents one pillar of a longhouse, creating a stable structure. These values are woven together so intimately that the strength and weakness of one affects each of the others.

Our ancestors, with the help of the Creator, formed our land base, language, laws, teachings and stories, songs and dances, clothing, ceremonies, traditions, and ways of life. We trained up our children to take care of their families and villages, and our elders provided sacred teachings and spiritual guidance. We manipulated the land through careful stewardship, and we influenced our territory and others around us through alliances and wars. Our chieftain lineage passed from oldest son to oldest son, and our women provided stability and grounding for our sacred ways.

Over time, we have evolved alongside the governments and cultures surrounding us. Canoes gave way to motorized vessels and vehicles; modern technology led to electricity, running water, and other tools that make our lives efficient. Our governmental structure turned away from the chieftain line and evolved to the elected leadership of both men and women. We continue to make our sacred regalia, harvest cedar logs and bark, travel in our canoes for ceremony, grow and harvest our traditional foods, and reach for economic opportunities that come from Western influence such as hotels, golf courses, and broadband operations. We protect our people and lands with a balanced blend of Indigenous and Western knowledge perspectives; traditional knowledge, contemporary science, data and reporting, and partnerships with Native and non-Native agencies are imperative to our continued expression of sovereignty—and our success as a people.

These values and philosophies are passed down generationally from our ancestral chiefs, and they run through the veins of our S'Klallam leaders today. W. Ron Allen, who has been Jamestown's chairman and CEO for over forty years, continues these teachings and makes them relevant to our contemporary times, saying, "We must coexist respectfully and responsibly." These beliefs bring traditional ethics into our governmental decision-making, our daily operations as a tribe, our young people's education, and our care for our people and lands. Our cultural and traditional values direct how we live life today and all generations to come.

yúčciʔə
Loni (Grinnell) Greninger, Prince Family
Vice Chairwoman, Jamestown S'Klallam Tribal Council

## nəxʷsƛ'áy'əm cə nəmá.
### The S'Klallam are a sacred, sovereign people.

Tribal nations are inherently sovereign; each tribe designs its own governmental structure, land base, culture, language, laws, and social structures. As the early explorers came to the North American continent, each tribe was viewed as a separate, sovereign governmental entity. The explorers, representing their own sovereign countries, signed legally binding agreements, called treaties, with the tribal nations. Each treaty described a trade agreement; for example, a tribe would give up a certain amount of their land in exchange for weapons, allied protection,

ongoing food supplies, and health care. Ideally, the treaty would benefit both parties equally. When the United States was born, the government followed suit in signing treaties with tribal nations. Land ownership was at the forefront of the new government's mind, as well as the new settlers who were excited to create a new home.

The S'Klallam were not immune to explorers and settlers moving west. Land ownership and remaining in one place year-round, as introduced by the Europeans, was a new concept for the S'Klallam. Traditionally, the S'Klallam traveled with the seasons and animal migration paths. By the 1850s, tension was growing between tribes and settlers. As a result, the Treaty of Point No Point of 1855 was signed by the S'Klallam, Skokomish, and Chemakum Nations and Isaac Stevens, the governor of Washington Territory. The treaty promised settlers millions of acres of land, and in return, it allowed the tribes to retain the rights to live according to their customs and receive health, education, and housing assistance from the federal government. After the treaty, the S'Klallam Nation was politically split by the federal and state government into three separate tribal nations. The Port Gamble S'Klallam Tribe became recognized by the federal government as sovereign in 1939. Some

years after, in 1968, the Lower Elwha Klallam Tribe became recognized as well. The Jamestown S'Klallam Tribe was last of the three "Sister Tribes" to be recognized on February 10, 1981. Today, the Sister Tribes remain in sovereign authority over their lands, resources, and people.

**Adapted from:** *Thirty Years and Time Immemorial: Commemorating the 30th Anniversary of the Official Federal Recognition of the Jamestown S'Klallam Tribe 1981–2011,* 2011. Authored by Betty Oppenheimer, communications specialist for the Jamestown S'Klallam Tribe.

### sčtə́ŋxʷən cə nəmá sčáʔčaʔɬ; sʔéŋaʔtəŋɬ. ʔaʔkʼʷə́ɬt st ʔiʔ ʔaʔkʷə́ɬtəŋ st.
### The earth is our sacred relative; the Creator gave us land. We protect it and it cares for us.

The area along the north shoreline of the Olympics, from the Hoko River to Discovery Bay and down Hood Canal to the Hamma Hamma River, remained S'Klallam territory until the increase of non-Native settlement a century later. The territory was dominated by geography, weather, and the available sea and land food resources. Fourteen hundred square miles of mountains overshadowed the

ABOVE **Mountain hemlocks on the slopes of Mount Ellinor overlook Lake Cushman, Hood Canal, and the Puget Sound lowlands.** OPPOSITE **Fall and winter rains swell the Hamma Hamma River at the southern end of traditional S'Klallam territory.**

Olympic Peninsula. Narrow lowlands hugged the shoreline and provided ideal winter and summer village sites where rivers and streams fell rapidly into the Strait of Juan de Fuca and Hood Canal. Over two hundred inches of rain fell annually on the highest peaks, but a rain shadow sheltered the Dungeness River area and resulted in a modest fifteen to twenty inches of rainfall a year.

The land, sea, and air provided for all the S'Klallam's needs. The plants and animals provided for ceremonial foods and regalia, the everyday diet and clothing, tools, weapons, shelter, and transportation. The S'Klallam considered the plants and animals to be brothers and sisters in creation. Because of this relationship, the S'Klallam studied the seasons and migrations of creation, and they knew when it was proper to harvest and when to let the land rest.

The majestic western redcedar trees were harvested to become family homes and community gathering spaces, canoes for water transportation and fishing, and tools such as fish clubs, and its bark was woven into clothing, baskets, and blankets. Available shellfish included cockles, various clams, mussels, oysters, crabs, and geoducks. Finfish such as salmon, halibut, dogfish, and lingcod were abundant in their seasons. On land, the S'Klallam harvested a broad variety of berries, flowers, leaves, bark, and roots. Additionally, animals provided for good protein, fats, furs, and bones for tools. Animals such as deer, bear, beaver, cougar, marmot, mink, muskrat, otter, rabbit, raccoon, wildcat, wolf, and panther were frequently hunted. The S'Klallam harvested an equally impressive array of birds including eagle, grouse, hawk, kingfisher, pheasant, quail, and woodpecker.

Adapted from: *The Jamestown S'Klallam Story*, 2002.
Authored by Joseph H. Stauss,
Jamestown S'Klallam tribal descendant.

## qʷáy st cə skʷáʔɬ sqʷáyɬ, nəxʷsʎ̕ayʼəmʼúcən.
## We speak our own language, S'Klallam/Klallam.

The S'Klallam language was entirely oral in nature before non-Natives began to study nəxʷsʎ̕ayʼəmʼúcən. All three Sister Tribes have been involved in language revitalization efforts for decades with the help of linguists and anthropologists. Their efforts kept the language from becoming extinct. The last fluent speaker was Adeline Smith, a tribal elder from the Lower Elwha Klallam Tribe who passed away in 2013.

Language revitalization efforts for the S'Klallam People began in 1847 with written phonetic recordings in English; as technology evolved, audio and video recordings were added. These recordings documented vocabulary, conversations, and songs. During the 1970s, Jamestown's attention shifted to the re-recognition of tribal sovereignty, self-governance, self-determination, and self-reliance. As was the case for many tribes, this new focus gave way to more efforts in economic development and Western higher education. After creating a strong economic and educational base for its citizens, in 2017 the Jamestown S'Klallam Tribe refocused on language revitalization efforts that continue today.

Hard work between the Sister Tribes and linguist Timothy Montler, PhD, led to a published Klallam dictionary in 2012. The 983-page book provides important acknowledgments of tribal elders, translations, an overview of the sounds in the language, and other aspects that are important in using the dictionary. In 2015, a companion Klallam grammar book was published, including sixty chapters of content that can train learners to converse, read, and write in the language. Today, the Sister Tribes have created their own community classes and resources. In addition, local school districts and colleges have adopted the S'Klallam language into their class listings, making the language available for any student, tribal and non-tribal, to learn. In exercising sovereignty, the Sister Tribes developed a S'Klallam/Klallam Language Board, which holds the authority to officially certify tribal citizens to teach the language within their communities or in local schools and colleges. In total, the Sister Tribes have over fifteen certified teachers and are working more closely than ever to train up more tribal citizens in the language.

Adapted from: *Klallam Grammar*, 2015.
Authored by Timothy Montler, PhD, linguist and
friend to the three S'Klallam/Klallam Sister Tribes.

OPPOSITE TOP LEFT **Community members net fish for surf smelt at Twin Beach on the Strait of Juan de Fuca.** OPPOSITE TOP RIGHT **Chris Burns, a natural resources technician with the Jamestown S'Klallam Tribe, hauls up his catch of surf smelt on Twin Beach on the Strait of Juan de Fuca.** OPPOSITE BOTTOM RIGHT **Surf smelt and oysters grill over an open fire.** OPPOSITE BOTTOM LEFT **Netting surf smelt as they spawn on the beach at high tide.**

# Rain, Rivers, and Redds

It happens almost overnight. The first scattered rains of September or October dampen forest floors and dust the mountains with snow. The change always grabs my attention, but clear autumn days of gold maples and migrating geese usually follow. Then, when jet stream and ocean conditions are right, an atmospheric river roars in from the tropical Pacific and breaks torrentially over the Olympic Mountains. The peninsula's rivers respond raucously.

I was camped with friends on the Hoh River in late October one year, lured by a lingering stretch of clear weather. Signs of fall were all about us. Fallen maple leaves covered the trail; mushrooms punched through patches of moss and needles. The faint bugling of elk signaled the rut was winding down, and the cool evening air had a bite. I remember sensing a change while crossing dry river channels to fetch water for dinner. Near dark, a fresh gust swept upvalley, sending willow and alder leaves spinning. We retreated to our tents early. That night it let loose.

I buried myself in my sleeping bag as wave after wave of heavy rain pounded the tent fly and the roar of the river grew. The next morning was a different world. Heavy clouds dragged at the ridges. Bare trees tossed in the wind. And the river, a quiet, distant stream just hours earlier, reclaimed its channels and churned whitely past our camp. Close to shore, where dry leaves and needles covered the river cobble the evening before, two large Chinook salmon, icons of these rain forest valleys, spawned vigorously in the current.

Largest of Pacific salmon, Chinook or king salmon weigh from fifteen to fifty pounds and spawn in the peninsula's major rivers. The female churned up long streamers of silt as she dug her nest, or redd, deep in river cobble with powerful kicks of her tail. The darker, hook-nosed male swam close beside her ready to fertilize hundreds to thousands of eggs. The fertile eggs will remain buried in gravel over the winter, bathed in the clean, oxygen-rich flow. Fry emerge in spring, and over the next few months they will work their way downstream to the ocean. There they range widely in the North Pacific, feeding and growing large and muscular for up to seven years before returning

to these same waters to spawn and die. With that final gesture, they—like all salmon—bequeath a generous bounty of nutrients from the ocean to the inland forest, nitrogen, phosphorous, and carbon among them.

Salmon are a critical link in the downstream flow of nutrients from mountains to sea. More than 130 wildlife species benefit from the seasonal gift of salmon to rivers, from bears to bald eagles, river otters to ravens, winter wrens to water shrews. Even streamside trees and shrubs garner nutrients from salmon carcasses dragged ashore by scavengers. Fallen leaf litter from salmon-enriched streamside trees in turn feeds aquatic invertebrates that young salmon depend upon for food. Large trees topple into rivers, creating pools where salmon can rest and take shelter from predators, riffles, spawning areas, and sources of aquatic insects. Fallen trees pile up into log jams that structure rivers, slow and spread floodwaters, and nourish floodplains. After the Ice Age, the return of forests to steep, glacier-scoured valleys transformed rivers, making them hospitable to salmon. Ever since, salmon have returned the favor.

Some seventy distinct stocks of wild Pacific salmon and steelhead ascend more than a dozen major river systems that radiate out from the Olympic Mountains. Olympic National Park, with four thousand miles of pristine rivers, streams, and large lowland lakes, is a sanctuary for wild salmon and steelhead unequalled in the coterminous United States. From glacier-fed headwaters through primeval forests to teeming estuaries, Olympic rivers and the thirty-one native fish species they harbor are a planetary treasure. Salmon embody the unity of mountain, forest, and ocean. For thousands of years these silver swimmers have provided sustenance for Native American cultures here. Although several stocks are threatened and currently managed under recovery plans, salmon remain at the center of the peninsula's identity, economy, and life.

Some Olympic salmon, such as those Chinook in the Hoh, are keyed to large, flood-prone rivers where they spawn in cobble-size gravel. Others, like chum salmon, return in large numbers to the peninsula's lower rivers. Pink salmon also spawn in lower rivers, but only in odd-numbered

A pair of Chinook salmon spawn in cobble-size gravel in the Elwha River. Chinook can spend as long as seven years at sea and historically reached large sizes in the Elwha.

years. Coho spawn in small streams, tributaries, and side channels throughout the peninsula; their fry remain in rivers for a year. Sockeye, rarest of Olympic salmon, spawn in river systems with large lakes: the Quinault, Ozette, and Elwha. Wild steelhead, feisty seagoing rainbow trout that venture far up Olympic rivers, attract sport fishers from around the world to cold winter streams. Another sea-run species, bull trout, has astounded biologists by visiting multiple rivers and habitats and also penetrating deep into the interior.

Until recently, the lives of salmon and other native fish were not well documented throughout peninsula rivers. With the removal of the Elwha dams on the horizon, park fisheries biologist Sam Brenkman saw an unprecedented opportunity to compare fish populations before and after dam removal. Working with a colleague who had pioneered surveys in Oregon rivers, they assembled twenty fisheries biologists to snorkel the length of the Elwha. They recorded every fish encountered: species and location. With most of the Elwha flowing through remote

wilderness accessible only by trail, logistics were a challenge. Camping equipment, snorkel gear, dry suits, wading boots, GPS systems, and laser range finders—some 1,200 pounds of gear—had to be packed in by mules. Camps were moved down valley daily as four teams snorkeled four to six miles of river per day.

Information gained during the first Elwha survey led Brenkman and colleagues to organize snorkel surveys of other Olympic rivers: the Quinault, Queets, South Fork Hoh, Bogachiel, Sol Duc, Skokomish, and the Elwha again after dam removal. Their goal is to create an atlas of peninsula riverscapes, the first of its kind. A dozen years and 420 river miles later, they're most of the way there. Data are collected by divers in pencil on arm-mounted PVC data plates, transferred to data sheets, and uploaded to produce detailed maps. Although fish-detecting technologies are becoming increasingly sophisticated, Brenkman believes nothing compares to hard data gathered by seasoned biologists in river environments. "Snorkeling is transformative," he told me. "It enables biologists to observe wild fish interacting in their home environments. Underwater, you see different species tucked in wood jams, hiding under large rocks, or jolting through pools and riffles. You realize how powerful and streamlined they are in their own environments, and how awkward we humans are in rivers by comparison."

RIGHT **The Glines Canyon Dam in Olympic National Park was one of two dams that blocked migratory fish from reaching spawning areas in the Elwha River watershed.** FAR RIGHT **Following the removal of the Elwha Dam in 2012 and the Glines Canyon Dam in 2014, salmon have been reclaiming their former territories.** OPPOSITE **A black bear catches salmon on the Hoh River in Olympic National Park. Fall salmon runs provide an important source of nutrients for black bears before winter hibernation.**

Other lives animate Olympic rivers. In spring, snow-melt rivers come to life when colorful harlequin ducks arrive from saltwater to nest along swollen streams. The only North American duck that breeds in steep mountain streams, harlequins surf rapids and scour the substrate for invertebrates, then rest and preen on mossy boulders. American dippers also haunt the white waters of the Olympics, bobbing on river rocks in their distinctive fashion. Dippers also feed on invertebrates and small fish. In summer I see them along the shores of mountain lakes and ponds. Farther downstream, belted kingfishers perch on overhanging limbs and dive expertly for small fish. Both birds reside here throughout the year. Mergansers, wood ducks, great blue herons, and green-winged teal frequent lower rivers; all benefit from the presence of salmon.

Throughout their range, wild salmon are at risk. Habit destruction from logging, damming, agricultural runoff, residential development, competition from hatchery fish, and overfishing at sea has been devastating to salmon. Today, only 5 to 7 percent of historic populations of wild Pacific salmon return to their rivers to spawn.

Nowhere on the peninsula was the loss of wild salmon to destructive development more poignant or more tragic than on the Elwha River. And nowhere has salmon recovery been more celebrated. Historically the Elwha supported ten distinct stocks including all species of Pacific salmon, steelhead, and char in numbers that approached four hundred thousand fish a year. The annual return of salmon to the river was an incredible year-round resource for the Elwha Klallam people and the entire watershed ecosystem. Elwha Chinook in particular were legendary for their size and robust strength. Yet two dams built in the early twentieth century completely blocked passage of salmon to all but the lower five miles of river. Fish returning to the Elwha dwindled to less than four thousand. Following decades-long efforts by the Lower Elwha Klallam Tribe, conservationists, salmon advocates, and government agencies, and with overwhelming popular support, legislation to restore the Elwha was passed by Congress, and both dams were taken down in 2012 and 2014.

Within months, coho, pink, and Chinook salmon and steelhead swam past the lower dam site. Sockeye, chum, and bull trout soon followed. When the upper dam came down, Chinook, steelhead, and bull trout penetrated the upper reaches of the river, with Chinook sighted thirty-six miles upstream from the mouth and bull trout even farther. Mountains of sediments trapped behind the dams were carried downstream by floods, replenishing spawning habitats in the lower river and rebuilding nearly one

hundred acres of estuary at the river mouth. Forage fish returned to the estuary as did flocks of gulls, cormorants, and other birds to feed on them. The dramatic recovery of the Elwha River ecosystem has just begun, but as the largest salmon restoration project in the Northwest, it has attracted visitors from around the world. Most importantly, it points the way toward future ecological restoration efforts and demonstrates how people of diverse backgrounds can work together to restore a damaged earth.

RIGHT **A great blue heron captures a meal.** OPPOSITE TOP LEFT **Male wood ducks may be the most handsome waterfowl on the peninsula. Wood ducks nest in tree cavities or nest boxes near forested wetlands, lakes, and rivers.** OPPOSITE TOP RIGHT **Brown pelicans visit the Olympic Peninsula in late spring and summer where they primarily fish the waters of the Pacific. They are seen in lesser numbers along the Strait of Juan de Fuca and Puget Sound.** OPPOSITE BOTTOM **Black oystercatchers are common residents of the peninsula's rocky intertidal areas where they feed on mussels, limpets, and other mollusks.**

TOP LEFT **An adult dunlin molting into breeding plumage forages during spring migration on the Washington coast.** TOP RIGHT **An immature peregrine falcon feeds on a freshly killed gull. Once endangered, peregrine falcons have recovered and were removed from the Endangered Species List in 1999.** BOTTOM **A pair of adult common mergansers rest on a moss-covered log.**

TOP LEFT **An American dipper pauses briefly on an alder limb. Dippers are emblematic of Olympic rivers; they live year-round in the upper reaches and feed primarily on aquatic insect larvae, gripping the substrate with their feet.** TOP RIGHT **Large, graceful trumpeter swans began wintering on the Olympic Peninsula in 1982. They have become one of the highlights of the peninsula's dark, rainy season.** BOTTOM **A pair of harlequin ducks feed among river rocks. One of the delights of spring on Olympic Peninsula rivers is the return of the harlequins that nest among fast-moving waters.**

ABOVE **Legendary kayaker Gary Korb takes on the summer rush of the upper Elwha River.** RIGHT **A fishing guide backs a drift boat into the Hoh River. Guided trips have become increasingly popular on the Peninsula's west-side rivers, which offer year-round fishing opportunities.** OPPOSITE LEFT **A fly fisherman tests the pristine waters of the Sol Duc River. With its high lakes, tributary creeks, and more than a dozen rivers flowing from the mountains, the Olympic Peninsula hosts more than thirty-seven species of native fish.** OPPOSITE RIGHT **A beautiful spawning coho salmon leaps upstream.**

# New Land: The Elwha Estuary

One of the most profound changes brought by dam removal on the Elwha River is best appreciated by closing your eyes. Stand at the river mouth and listen: there it is. The sound of waves on Washington's newest beach.

At the river mouth and along the Strait of Juan de Fuca, what had become a beach of bare, ankle-turning cobble has been transformed. From the crash of waves on rock, the music of the beach today is the silken *hush hush* of the tide, lapping soft sand.

Taking down two massive dams on the Elwha did more than open up the river for the migration of salmon for the first time in more than a hundred years. It also restarted the mighty conveyor belt of the Elwha, enabling it to once again transport big wood, sand, and gravel all the way from the mountains to the sea.

This is what mighty mountain rivers do as they continually rebuild the natural environment of their channel, mouth, beach, and nearshore. For more than a century on the Elwha, that crucial process was disrupted by the dams. The river and beach starved as two dams hoarded some twenty million cubic yards of sediment, sand, and gravel trapped in reservoirs. Beaches at the river mouth, including along the reservation of the Lower Elwha Klallam Tribe, were eroding at the rate of more than a foot per year—and that rate was accelerating, according to Jonathan Warrick of the US Geological Survey (USGS), who tracked the beach's changes before and after dam removal.

Dam removal began in September 2011. Six months later the Elwha Dam was gone, followed by the Glines Canyon Dam in 2014. Today, the Elwha River once again flows freely from its headwaters in the Olympic Mountains to the Strait of Juan de Fuca. No one knew how long it would take the Elwha to spit out the massive slug of sediment released from behind the dams—the equivalent of two million dump truck loads. That, according to USGS, is on the order of a sediment dump from the eruption of a moderately sized volcano.

Most of the sediment released was coarse sand, gravel, and cobble, while 37 percent of it was silt and clay. The river worked ceaselessly and efficiently at transporting about 90 percent of the sediment behind the dams, some thirty million tons of it, all the way to saltwater. The result is new land. According to a paper published by USGS, the amount of beach area on the Elwha increased by 173 percent, river bars by 480 percent, and river mouth bars by 567 percent.

All those physical changes detonated an equally big biological response. A wholesale turnover of the suite of life at the river mouth and nearshore is still in the works, moving toward a community of plants and animals more like what was there before the hydroelectric dams were built beginning in 1910. Kelp beds once offshore of the river mouth are gone in a full-on "kelpocalypse." Wholesale change in the substrate on the seabed is the reason. Kelp has holdfasts at the base of the plant that cling to bare cobble on the seabed. But that cobble was buried in wave after wave of soft sand carried down to saltwater by the river.

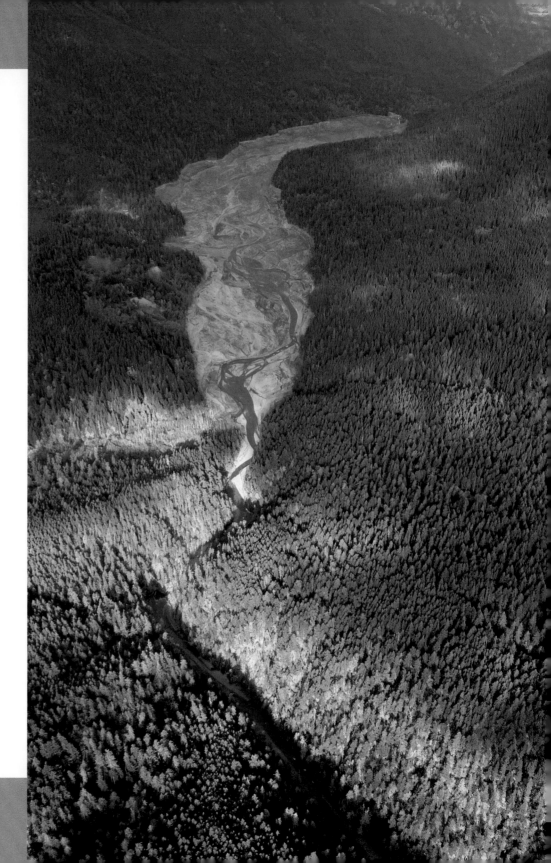

That transformation opened the door for colonization of the soft, sandy bottom by sand lance, an important forage fish. Sand lance are a crucial food for seabirds, salmon, and other wildlife. Dam removal on the Elwha has even helped in the recovery of endangered southern resident orcas. The orcas eat Chinook salmon, which fatten on forage fish.

Lower Elwha Klallam tribal members also are enjoying the first crab fishery at the river mouth in generations. The return of a productive Dungeness crab fishery along the Elwha delta is all the more important as the tribe continues to forebear in not exercising its treaty-protected fishing rights in the Elwha so as to give fish runs time to rebuild. That's a process that managers estimate will take from twenty to forty years—which may sound like a long time, but if anything, scientists have been surprised at how quickly the Elwha is recovering.

To walk the beach today is to realize with your own eyes and ears that change is possible—and can be even bigger and faster than anyone expected. In this way, the Elwha is an inspiration not only here at home but also around the world, wherever human alterations of rivers has harmed native ecologies and cultures.

All dams eventually fill with sediment. Where dam removal is the right choice, the Elwha shows rivers can rebound toward abundance and health.

—Lynda V. Mapes

RIGHT **The gravel bed of the former Lake Mills reservoir in Olympic National Park following the removal of the Glines Canyon Dam. Some thirty million tons of sediments, sand, and gravel, trapped behind the two Elwha River dams, are now revitalizing the Elwha estuary, beaches, and nearshore areas.** OPPOSITE **Following dam removal, the mouth of the Elwha River was transformed by river-deposited sediments, long held back by dams, into a species-rich delta.**

**A clear day in winter on the Quinault River in Olympic National Park**

# Quinault Worldview

*Gary Morishima, Quinault Indian Nation*

## The Past Is Prologue

The Olympic Peninsula came to be through forces of shifting continents, volcanic eruptions, wind, water, fire, and evolving life-forms. In terms of geologic age, it is a baby, created by ecological processes that began about two and a half million years ago. As glaciers formed and melted, archaeological evidence verifies that people learned to adapt and have survived here for at least thirteen thousand years.

Quinaults lived in the largest tribal community on the southwest part of the peninsula, Kwi'nail. They were peoples of the land and sea who travelled to hunt, fish, and gather from the mountains to ocean waters far offshore. The rivers, the arteries and veins of the earth that brought nourishment and cleansed the land, were also highways. Salmon returned in such abundance that the thunderous noise of fish swimming upstream announced their arrival. The tree of life, western redcedar, provided fuel, clothing, shelter, and materials for artistic expression as well as for canoes and paddles for travel and trade. Abundant foods and medicines from the forest, beaches, ocean, and prairies were harvested and shared.

But Quinaults were more than takers. They served as stewards of the land, the waters, and their relatives, caring for all things that walk, swim, fly, or grow roots to sustain their bodies, spirits, culture, and economy for those to come. Lessons learned were passed from generation to generation as traditional knowledge and wisdom through language, customs, songs, dances, stories, ceremonies, and practices. In today's vernacular, the relationship between the Quinaults and their environment is termed a "social-economic-ecological system." But to the Quinaults, it is simply a relationship of oneness with their environment grounded in a worldview of interdependence, interconnectedness, and humility that has both spiritual and metaphysical dimensions. It is a relationship based on reciprocity and respect: they care for the land so it can care for them in return. A poem written by Clarence Pickernell, known affectionately as "Teach," reflects a Quinault worldview of moral responsibility and a covenant with the generations to follow:

> This is my land.
> From the time of the first moon
> Till the time of the last sun. It was given to my people.
> Wha-neh, the great giver of life,
> Made me out of the earth of this land.
> He said, "You are the land and the land is you."
> I take good care of this land,
> For I am part of it.
> I take good care of the animals,
> For they are my brothers and sisters.
> I take care of the streams and rivers,
> For they clean my land.
> I honor Ocean as my father,
> For he gives me food and a means of travel.
> Ocean knows everything, for he is everywhere.
> Ocean is wise, for he is old.
> Listen to Ocean, for he speaks wisdom.
> He sees much, and knows more.
> He says, "Take care of my sister Earth.
> She is young and has little wisdom, but much kindness.
> When she smiles, it is springtime.
> Scar not her beauty, for she is beautiful beyond all things.
> Her face looks eternally upward to the beauty of sky
>     and stars, where once she lived with her father, Sky."
> I am forever grateful for this beautiful and
>     bountiful earth.
> God gave it to me.
> This is my land.

Quinault tribal member Dino Blackburn pulls salmon in with his gillnet on the Chehalis River.

From the time that British naval captain John Meares christened Mount Olympus in 1788, the dense rain forests, snowcapped mountain range, rivers, and ocean beaches teeming with fish and wildlife have been reminiscent of a special, heavenly place recorded in the mythologies of ancient Greece. The audacity! European explorers presumed that the claim of discovery, sanctioned by sixteenth-century papal bulls *Dum Diversas* and *Inter Caetera,* gave them the right to name and take places without regard, consideration, or even recognition that the land was already occupied by non-Christian "pagans" for many thousands of years before the countries asserting possession had been formed.

It is not possible to delve into the details and complex history of Indian law and the nuances of tribal-federal-state relations within the scope of this chapter; however, a few salient points are necessary to provide some context and understanding of Quinault relationships with the Olympic Peninsula.

In 1855, Quinault ancestors entered into a treaty with the United States, ceding claims to millions of acres of the territory they occupied in exchange for promises that a reservation would be set aside for their exclusive use and occupancy and that their ability to fish, hunt, and gather would forever be protected. Within a few short years, treaty promises began to be ignored as the land was opened for settlement and development. Soon after Washington gained statehood, it began to pass laws and issue regulations that discriminated against Indian fishing. When the Quinault Reservation was established, a boundary survey error wrongfully excluded fifteen thousand acres to protect claims by homesteaders. In the early 1900s, Congressional action was pursued to try to gain control over Lake Quinault to promote recreation and development. The lands set aside for Quinault use were decimated by the 1887 Dawes Act, which authorized the division of Indian reservations into eighty-acre parcels held in trust by the United States for individuals in an attempt to force Indians to abandon their communal lifestyles and become assimilated into the European-based societal mainstream as farmers while paving the way to transfer ownership to non-Indians. By 1933, the entire reservation had been allotted, leaving Quinaults without a communal homeland. Over time, allotment ownership became increasingly complex and alienated through processes of inheritance, impeding and increasing the expense of resource management.

Quinaults were displaced from other parts of their traditional territories by other federal actions. Theodore Roosevelt established Mount Olympus National Monument in 1909; Franklin Roosevelt re-designated it as a national park in 1938; and UNESCO then named the park a Biosphere Reserve in 1976 and a World Heritage Site in 1981. More recently, Congress included 95 percent of the park as part of the Olympic Wilderness Area. While these actions furthered public use and enjoyment, they also fostered conflict by largely rendering moot treaty reserved rights. Policies and politics of "conservation" here were rooted in impalpable notions of eugenics, racial superiority, denigration of tribal knowledge, and exclusion of the peoples who had cared for the land and its resources for countless generations.

During the span of just a few decades, the tribal peoples who had made their homes on the peninsula were deprived of the ability to assert power and influence. As settlement progressed, their communities were devastated by the introduction of new diseases brought by traders, explorers, and settlers. Laws prevented tribal members from voting. Children were removed from their homes and placed in boarding schools. Alien systems of governance and commerce undermined the foundations and fabric of the Quinault societal structure. A complex and ever-changing web of unfamiliar laws, rules, regulations, and policies disrupted Quinault relationships with their environment and their neighbors. The imposition of European-based socio-economic-legal systems brought unfamiliar concepts of property ownership, fragmented jurisdiction, and narrow, siloed thinking that led to the deterioration of ecological functions and the resources that had been central to Quinault society. Tribal tenets of sustainable use and communal sharing were displaced by consumption, endless growth, and accrual of individual wealth.

By the early 1900s, loggers coveted the dense evergreen forests of the Quinault Reservation for timber. Billions of board feet were harvested by rail and trucks. One-log loads from huge spruce trees were used to manufacture a wide variety of products ranging from warplanes to sounding boards for pianos. Shiploads of western redcedar logs were exported. After the Bureau of Indian Affairs (BIA), the principal agency responsible for administering the Indian trust estate for the United States, decided to offer Quinault timber north of the Quinault River in three large units to minimize administrative costs and the challenges of negotiating timber sales on individual allotments, collusion followed. The Taholah and Crane Creek Units each received only a single bid while the third, the Queets Unit, received none at all, leaving the area accessible for timber harvest by smaller companies. A 1956 General Accounting Office audit indicated below-market stumpage rates were being charged for the Taholah and Crane Creek Units. Clearcutting left mountains of slash on tens of thousands of acres from high-grading and the intentional breakage of less valuable timber. There was no reforestation, and no seed sources were left to allow for natural regeneration in the few spots where bare ground was accessible. Salmon habitats were destroyed as streams were choked with sediment and logjams. During the Termination Era of federal policy of the 1950s and 1960s, the BIA pursued supervised sales of allotments to try to divest the United States of its trust responsibilities.

The scandalous history of timberlands was investigated by Congress, spurred litigation, and even included a nefarious money laundering scheme to secure loans for arms sales in the Iran-Contra Affair. The forests, waters, salmon, wildlife, and traditional foods and medicines suffered under federal mismanagement. The islands offshore didn't escape either; they were used by the military as bombing ranges.

To heighten awareness of the damage done to its reservation, Quinault closed its beaches to the public to prevent encroachment and desecration of sacred sites. To protest liquidation of tens of thousands of acres of forest, logging roads were blockaded and litigation was filed against the United States for mismanagement. The resulting series of Supreme Court decisions in the Mitchell cases established liability of the United States for breaching fiduciary trust obligations.

Quinault did not just complain or sue, it took action to try to correct problems and make things better. When the 1975 Indian Self-Determination and Education Assistance Act (ISDEAA) was passed, Quinault quickly began to develop its own program to remediate damage and proactively manage reservation forest land. To counter the BIA's recalcitrance in accepting tribal efforts to assume greater responsibility for forest management, Secretary of the Interior Cecil Andrus was convinced to conduct a site visit to witness firsthand the existing problems and the vision of Quinault leadership's efforts to rehabilitate the reservation's forests.

Quinault played a pivotal role in the 1974 United States v. Washington case, popularly known as the "Boldt Decision," which affirmed and defined the nature of reserved Indian treaty fishing rights and the ability of tribes to become self-regulating, free of state interference absent demonstration of a conservation necessity under conditions specified by the Supreme Court. Following that decision, Quinault was instrumental in countering the backlash of anti-Indian treaty abrogation scapegoating, pressing for passage of the 1980 Salmon and Steelhead Conservation and Enhancement Act to lay a foundation for addressing long-standing environmental and management problems responsible for the decline of fishery resources.

Over time, the salmon returning to rivers of the Washington coast, Puget Sound, and the Columbia Basin that had sustained tribal communities for thousands of years were reduced to a small fraction of their former abundance as habitats deteriorated from development and impacts from fisheries off the coasts of Canada and Alaska. Communities dependent on tribal, commercial, and recreational fisheries suffered dire consequences. Understanding that this problem was beyond the ability of Quinault alone to resolve, tribal leadership took legal, administrative, and political actions to develop coalitions

OPPOSITE **A clearcut in Olympic National Forest. The 1994 Northwest Forest Plan reformed forest management in Olympic National Forest. Clearcutting is no longer practiced in Olympic National Forest but is standard practice on other industrial forest lands.**

and forge partnerships to convince Canada and the United States to adopt the 1985 Pacific Salmon Treaty to reduce interceptions by Canadian and Alaskan fisheries and increase coordinated, multijurisdictional management.

Quinault has been a leader in promoting and advancing natural resource management locally, nationally, and internationally. Recognizing that individual tribal governments would have little power to effect the changes needed to improve management of natural resources, Quinault embarked upon national efforts to defeat a "divide and conquer" strategy that had been long pursued by industry, federal, state, and local governments by pushing for a unified tribal voice and cooperative actions to remediate and improve management of Indian natural resources, helping to found the Intertribal Timber Council and the National Tribal Environmental Council. At the state level, Quinault played a pivotal role in developing the Centennial Accord between Washington State and tribal governments; the Timber, Fish, and Wildlife Agreement; and the Climate Commitment Act. Quinault pushed for important national legislation, including the National Indian Forest Resources Management Act to codify the trust responsibility of the United States, the Tribal Forest Protection Act, the Tribal Self-Governance Program, the Indian Trust Asset Reform Act, and various tribal amendments to Farm Bill authorities. Quinault leaders served in prominent positions within regional and national tribal organizations, including the Affiliated Tribes of Northwest Indians, National Tribal Leaders Association, and National Congress of American Indians.

To provide a secure homeland and counter adverse rulings of the US Supreme Court that conditioned tribal sovereignty on land ownership, Quinault leadership secured the support of Senator Daniel Evans to pass the North Boundary Act to restore several thousand acres of the reservation that had been erroneously excluded by a boundary survey error, utilize revenues from timber sales for land consolidation, and improve forest management. An aggressive land acquisition program has now enabled the Quinault Indian Nation to gain ownership of over 40 percent of the reservation.

Environmental degradation caused by non-Indian development and resource extraction practices led to the restriction of Quinault access and use of natural resources due to concerns over species listed under the Endangered Species Act. Quinault pursued litigation against the US Department of the Interior for restrictions on timber harvests imposed on North Boundary lands for the protection of the marbled murrelet under threat from widespread logging of federal and private forests throughout its range that had begun in the nineteenth century (ultimately settled by the United States' agreement to purchase perpetual conservation easements). In addition, Quinault helped forge a coalition that led to an order signed by the Secretaries of Interior and Commerce entitled "American Indian Tribal Rights, Federal-Tribal Trust Responsibilities, and the Endangered Species Act." Quinault was also instrumental in revising the US Fish and Wildlife Service's Native American Policy and the US Forest Service's Tribal Relations Program to provide guidance for federal agencies in their administration of their responsibilities to consider impacts on tribal communities as they manage natural resources.

The most formidable challenges confronting the Quinaults today are not economic or political, but rather environmental. Salmon, which sustained Quinault culture and economy for countless generations, are now especially vulnerable to the impacts of environmental change. Because of their anadromous, semelparous life histories, salmon species are susceptible to accelerating changes in precipitation and temperature that affect both freshwater and marine environments. For example, Quinault blueback salmon depend upon clean, cold water for spawning in the area above Lake Quinault and rearing in Lake Quinault. The glacier that had provided water for spawning salmon over hundreds of centuries is disappearing, melting as temperatures increase and precipitation patterns change. The Quinaults made the extraordinarily difficult decision to close the Quinault River and Lake Quinault to fishing when the blueback spawning run declined precipitously. The tribe embarked upon a multidecade effort in partnership with state, federal, and conservation groups to

remediate damage from logging and recreational development by placing engineered logjams designed to encourage the reestablishment of forested islands to reduce erosion potential and restore historic flow patterns and ecological processes.

In just a blink of geologic time, anthropogenic industrialization, development, and population growth have ushered in an accelerating pace of change. The internet and social media have drastically altered how we inform our decisions and relate to one another. Diaspora is bringing new neighbors and different species are displacing old. Technology and development are altering our understandings, relationships with the environment, and utilization of resources. The productivity, phenology, and distribution of flora and fauna that has long sustained tribal communities are being affected by pharmaceuticals, chemicals, plastics, and global warming. Ecological, economic, and social systems are being disrupted. Scarcity and competition are replacing normative behavior based on abundance and sharing.

Quinault leadership has actively and aggressively pursued efforts to address climate change, human rights, and environmental justice in national and international processes for several years. It has been both proactive and reactive, embarking upon a project to relocate villages from low-lying areas along the Pacific coast to higher ground to reduce threats from storm surge, sea level rise, and tsunamis.

Quinault developed tribal forestry and fisheries programs that provide stewardship practices that combine both Western science and traditional knowledge. Its forestry programs include efforts to contend with water stress, insects, disease, and wildfire. Quinault land consolidation efforts are built on tenets of active forest management and long-term resilience to environmental stressors. Its marine fisheries programs include efforts to monitor and address harmful algal blooms, hypoxia events, and invasive species. Quinault has fought tenaciously to be recognized as a comanager of shared natural resources with the state of Washington and the federal government. Quinault also has partnered with a range of local private and public groups, as well as actively participated in multijurisdictional processes like those of the Northwest Indian Fisheries Commission, Pacific Fishery Management Council, Pacific Salmon Commission, International Pacific Halibut Commission, Intertribal Timber Council, and Olympic National Marine Sanctuary.

Quinault has long recognized that the key to its future lies in its ability to exercise its rights of self-determination and has steadfastly resisted efforts to dismiss or diminish its sovereignty. States have attempted to attack and diminish tribal jurisdiction and sovereignty by asserting claims of state's rights in state and federal courts. The Quinaults have been forced to contend with the BIA and a jurisdictional legal morass that diminished tribal sovereign authorities for decades.

Quinault took the step of recording its own bylaws in written form in 1922, and it pressed for increased tribal administration of programs for its communities under the ISDEAA and adoption of tribal self-governance to expand the ability of tribal governments to manage their own programs. When challenges to tribal management authority and sovereignty arose during the mid-1970s, bylaws were revised to adopt the present-day moniker of Quinault Indian Nation and codify a right of membership to individuals with a combined one-quarter heritage of tribes that received allotments on the reservation. It also began to assume its current form of governance, establishing departments for health care, education, social services, natural resources, and public safety to provide governmental services and fulfill responsibilities.

To protect and restore the health and productivity of natural resources of the Olympic Peninsula, Quinault has asserted its inherent sovereignty, treaty rights, and federal trust responsibilities to fend off efforts to build oil terminals, potash facilities, and recreational developments that would pollute the waters and beaches of the Olympic Peninsula. Quinault has opposed efforts to construct a dam on the Chehalis River that would harm treaty-protected rights to fish, hunt, and gather cultural resources; it has worked instead to collaboratively develop a dual approach that can both reduce damage from flooding and restore the abundance and productivity of aquatic species.

Maintaining environmental stewardship has been the central goal and focus for Quinault. Asserting sovereign authority to undo a century of policy, programs, and court decisions aimed at erasing and dispossessing tribal peoples has not been easy. During the course of the history of

OPPOSITE TOP **Ocean waves sweep up on the beach to the seawall and the town of Taholah on the Quinault Indian Reservation. Taholah, like many coastal communities, is at a high risk of flooding due to sea-level rise.** OPPOSITE BOTTOM **A portion of Taholah's relocation site, safe from sea-level rise**

the United States, administrative policies and laws have ignored tribal rights and sovereignty. Enduring decades of efforts to erase its very being, the Quinaults are finding ways to reassert their sovereignty and their presence.

Quinaults understand that there is little to be gained by lamenting or dwelling on the multigenerational trauma suffered in the past. While it is important to remember, they know that the task at hand is to make decisions and take actions today that will protect and advance the interests of the generations yet unborn.

In these times when the accelerating pace of global climate change threatens the very ability of humanity to survive, there is growing interest in the value of the place-based knowledge and wisdom found in tribal communities.

A century and a half of imposed policies rooted in an ethos of colonialism and exploitation, dispossession, and disenfranchisement has left behind a detritus of impacts on the environment and torn asunder the social fabric of tribal communities. Environmental laws and agreements intended to reverse some of these impacts have been garnering more attention in recent years, but it will take more than rules and regulatory frameworks to sustain a healthy planet. Fortunately, the public is now becoming increasingly aware of the rights of Indigenous peoples and the need to provide just treatment and to understand, share, and work in common purpose with neighbors near and far. Indigenous peoples have much to offer and contribute. It is vital for tribal peoples and their holistic worldviews of

LEFT **The Generations House is a multiuse community building in the Quinault Nation dedicated to elders and children. The new building is on an elevated relocation site for the town of Taholah.** OPPOSITE **Guy McMinds helped develop the Quinault Natural Resources program and became its first director. He is pictured here in a forest stand on the Quinault Indian Reservation. McMinds passed away in 2021.**

interconnectedness to have a prominent place at the table and to help find a path that will lead to a tomorrow where we can all live and thrive.

A transilience in ethical thinking, morality, vision, and worldview is needed. Imagine how much of the environmental damage we contend with today might have been reduced, mitigated, or even avoided if only the wisdom of sustainable use held by the first stewards of this land had been heeded. The tribal ethos of stewardship and humility now needs to displace Western hubris and dominance of the environment.

The focus on responsibility for environmental stewardship remains paramount. Honor the past, embrace the present, and do the utmost to heal, care for, and create a better future for the small part of our world known as the Olympic Peninsula so all can be blessed with its gifts. Guy McMinds, a Quinault leader in natural resources, expressed the importance of environmental relationships in a way that echoes Teach's words—from the time of the first moon, till the time of the last sun—"The roots of the Quinault Indian Nation lie deep within the land. The land and its resources represent both our heritage from the past and our legacy for the future."

The Quinault Indian Nation continues to evolve as it contends with legal, economic, and political challenges; vagaries of federal policy; broken promises; and shocking duplicity. Their story is one of adaptation, vision, persistence, determination, healing, and action to assume the responsibility to serve as agents of change. The past is prologue; the future is a work in progress.

## Destruction and Renewal at the Ocean's Edge

The soft thunder of breakers carries through the trees and quickens our pace as friends and I hike the Third Beach trail. By the time we scramble over silver-gray driftwood logs to the beach, gull cries vie with the surf. The tide is in, and footprints are few on the washed sand. White-caps pitch against the shore and collapse into sheets of foam that race across the beach in windswept banners. The sky is overcast, the air cool, and though we're still a week shy of the equinox, it's now official. For our small group making its yearly pilgrimage to the coast, spring has begun.

Even as winter lies low and gray as a wet blanket over the peninsula, spring utters its first gold-green murmurings along the outer coast. Green spears sprout from flattened tufts of grass on headlands, blunt buds of coltsfoot nose through fallen alder leaves, and bright bracts of skunk cabbage blunder up through the mud. It's all a tonic to us. For forty years or more, the same dogged group of old peninsula friends gather at La Push for a few quietly adventurous days of coast hiking, wildlife viewing, card games, and potluck dinners. We're writers, fishermen, carpenters,

musicians, tree planters, teachers, and artists—all united by decades of friendship and our shared love for this place. Kids and grandkids have grown and moved on, but we return year after year. It's become a spring rite for us.

Today, a group of us head south from Third Beach toward Strawberry Point. A pair of bald eagles circles over the coastal spruces, and crows rasp from wind-sculpted alders. Soon, eagles will return in numbers to their nests high in the spruces. Remote and undeveloped, the seventy or more miles of Olympic coast provide some of the most productive bald eagle nesting areas in the United States. The coast is a haven for other iconic birds as well, peregrine falcons, marbled murrelets, and brown pelicans among them. As spring returns to these coastal waters, more than one hundred thousand pairs of seabirds—puffins, murres, auklets, cormorants, storm-petrels, and gulls—flock to the offshore rocks. There, on more than 870 islands and sea stacks protected by the Washington Islands National Wildlife Refuges, they will nest and rear their young.

The sheer effusiveness of life born of this mingling of rivers, forest, rocks, and sea has created a realm of unparalleled biological richness and timeless beauty. With every dawn the beach is newly washed, but for tracks left by river otters or raccoons on nightly forays. As early mist lifts through coastal trees, earth and sea seem newly made.

A storm had moved through, and the booming surf still carries a bass note of winter. Harsh weather rakes the coast from November through February, sometimes later, and when storms ride in on the backs of the highest winter tides, the results are dramatic. Wind and rain pummel the forest, whipping trees like stalks of wheat. Waves hammer headlands and send driftwood logs tumbling in the surf. Creeks run both ways with the swells.

Following the beach south, the signs of winter storms are ever present. Waves wash the tops of wind-felled spruces, and hillsides of alders sprawl in heaps where they slid from rain-saturated bluffs. Driftwood logs are scattered and restacked like loosely flung cordwood, while other parts of the beach are swept clean. When we reach the bluff at Taylor Point, the fixed rope to the headland trail is buried in a rubble of rocks and mud.

ABOVE **Spotting a tufted puffin is a highlight of a visit to the Olympic coast. They nest on offshore islands in spring and summer; they winter at sea. Puffin populations have been in steep decline in their southern range from British Columbia to California, but the reasons for this decline have not been clearly determined.** OPPOSITE **Conspicuous and pungent skunk cabbage is one of the first signs of spring to adorn the peninsula's coastal lowlands.**

Felled trees and washed-out bluffs are merely the surface whittlings of a ceaseless carving of land by the sea. Driven by yearly cycles of Pacific storms and charged with the explosive power of wind-driven waves, hurled logs, and trapped air, the ocean has sculpted a seascape of spectacular contrasts. Rugged buttresses of rocky headlands, along with scattered islands, sea stacks, arches, and tunnels punctuate the outer coast. Long stretches of gravel and cobble beach rattle in wave wash, and sandy shores to the south are churned and smoothed by tides. Each of these habitats support their own suites of robust life forms.

After a short climb, we settle into a high perch on the headland overlooking a blue-green expanse of sea and sky. A waterfall shakes itself loose from the windy cliff below us, and waves ruffle whitely against dark offshore rocks. With thermoses of tea close at hand, we begin another spring rite: watching for northing whales.

Each February, gray whales set out on the longest migratory journey of any mammal on earth. Thousands of them follow an ancient route along the coast from winter calving areas in Baja to summer feeding grounds in the Arctic. Other baleen whales—minke, fin, blue, and northern right whales—ply Washington's offshore waters, along with several species of porpoises and dolphins. But these are usually well offshore and not easily seen from the coast. The grays' spring migrations bring them, and sometimes humpbacks, close by the peninsula's shores. Each spring we watch for their spray plumes rising like puffs of cloud above the waves.

For the Makah and other Native people of the Northwest coast, whales represent the lifeblood of their cultures. Traditionally, whales provided sustenance, social organization, wealth, and spiritual strength. The Makah, Quileute, Hoh, and Quinault people maintain an ongoing relationship with the ocean world and the creatures that dwell here. While my friends and I visit, tribal people know the coast as home.

Some of us decide to head back up the beach while a few stalwarts, Ray, Jimmy, Thomas, Chuck, and I, continue south. We keep an eye out for the elusive grays but also scan offshore kelp forests for another sea mammal that has swum back from the edge of extinction, the sea otter. Farther south we spot a few. They float high in a kelp bed, buoyed by air they blow into their lustrous dark fur, and begin to groom. It is a delight to spy on them with binoculars. They twist and turn somersaults in the low swells, puff up their thick undercoats, and scrub themselves vigorously. Lacking an insulating layer of blubber, they tend their coats religiously. Ironically, it was the warm, luxuriant quality of their fur that led to their extirpation from the Northwest coast. Fur traders hunted them ruthlessly and effectively in the eighteenth and nineteenth centuries. By the early 1900s, otters were eliminated from most of their Pacific range. In the 1970s, sea otters from Alaska were reintroduced to the Olympic coast, and today the population has bounded back to more than three thousand. By keeping sea urchin numbers in check, they nurture the growth of offshore kelp forests and thus ensure habitats for a wide variety of fish and other marine organisms, from skeleton shrimps to sea birds and salmon.

Sea otters and harbor seals are the only sea mammals known to breed and live year-round off the Olympic coast. As we hike past the offshore rocks of Giant's Graveyard,

I spot the familiar silver-gray shapes of dozens of harbor seals asleep on low reefs in the lee of some islands. Soon elephant seals will arrive from their breeding grounds in California and Mexico, and fur seals will swim south from Alaska to join the seasonal feast. In late summer, large numbers of California sea lions arrive from southern breeding grounds; larger Steller's sea lions from farther north will also come to feed in these coastal waters.

Cormorants fly low back and forth over the nearshore swells, and bright orange-beaked oystercatchers probe seaweed-covered rocks for limpets and chitons in the outgoing tide. More than one hundred species of marine and shorebirds benefit from the incredible richness of this coast. Many, like common murres, tufted puffins, and rhinoceros auklets, nest on islands and sea stacks. Many more visit these rich marine waters in summer. The Olympic Coast National Marine Sanctuary was established to study and conserve this incredible biological bounty in partnership with the first stewards of this place, the tribes.

By mid-afternoon the tide is out. Ray, Jimmy, Thomas, and Chuck become lost in a tide pool, while I venture onto a rocky point where exposed reefs are accessible. I watch my step on some slippery rockweed, hop-skipping over dense beds of night-blue mussels and patches of crusty barnacles, and scan the water's edge for beach crabs and whelks. On the far shore of the island off Strawberry Point, a series of channels and pools stretches invitingly toward the swells.

The range and diversity of intertidal life on the Olympic coast is stunning. Conspicuous ochre sea stars and slender red-orange blood stars clamp to the sides of rocks and channels. Flowerlike, translucent green and red-striped sea anemones wave sticky tentacles in the current. A bug-eyed sculpin holds still in a tide pool. As I push aside blades of sea grass, a miniature reddish-pink forest of coralline algae appears, and within it a tiny iridescent brooding anemone the color of a pearl.

Lying midway between northern and southern ranges and harboring species common to Alaska as well as southern California, Olympic intertidal areas support a phenomenal diversity of plants and animals, even greater

A gray whale sounds and dives with the Olympic Mountains in the distance.

TOP Steller's sea lions arrive on the Olympic coast in late summer. Larger than their cousins the California sea lions, they breed in more northern waters but commonly feed and haul-out on the peninsula's offshore rocks and islands. Tatoosh Island off Cape Flattery on the Makah Reservation is a favored haul out. BOTTOM In spring, bald eagles court, mate, nest, and rear young along the peninsula's coastal areas. Once listed as threatened under the Endangered Species Act, bald eagles have made a remarkable recovery. OPPOSITE TOP Humpback whales are bubble-net feeders. They circle schools of small fish such as salmon, krill, or herring and trap them in a "net" of blown bubbles. They then swim upward, mouths open, and feed on the trapped prey. OPPOSITE RIGHT Humpback whales are large (up to sixty feet or more) baleen whales with grooved underbellies and long pectoral fins. They live in all oceans and are seen regularly off the Olympic coast. OPPOSITE LEFT Gray whales migrate north from their calving areas in Baja and are seen along the Olympic coast in spring. Removed from the Endangered Species List in 1994 and considered recovered, their numbers have begun declining again in recent years.

than the inland forest ecosystem. Rivers deliver a continuous infusion of nutrients to coastal waters. Seasonal offshore currents and winds churn these cold nutrient-laden waters up to sunlit regions where they nurture thick blooms of microscopic plankton, the basis for all marine life. Nutrients foster a lush growth of seaweeds as well as a plethora of marine animals that feed on and in them. Mild, fog-tempered summers and relatively warm, temperate winters optimize growth.

Like plants of the inland mountains, plants and animals of the rocky shore also occupy well-defined zones. The high tide zone harbors tough acorn barnacles, limpets, snails, and shore crabs. Sea moss, sea lettuce, and rockweed also do well in the high tide zone. Just below, the middle intertidal area is a realm of seaweeds and dense beds of California mussels. Fleshy seaweeds like sea cabbage and sea sac can retain moisture while exposed to air. With the exception of two sea grasses, all seaweeds are algae; they attach to the substrate with tough, fist-like holdfasts and absorb sunlight and nutrients through leaflike blades. More than 130 species have been identified in Olympic National Park's intertidal area. Their diversity and abundance increases with depth below high tide. As I explore the outer edge of a sea stack, I find a stand of stout, shaggy-topped sea palms. Because these plants thrive on the most exposed, wave-blasted rocks, I keep a close eye on the changing tide.

Blue-black bands of California mussels cover the mid-surfaces of the rocks, giving way along the steepest sides to the white segmented shells of gooseneck barnacles. Smaller blue mussels are more common in the lee of rocks and islands. Mussels would dominate middle and lower intertidal zones but for another pervasive intertidal inhabitant, the ochre sea star.

The stout, five-armed sea star *Pisaster* ranges in color from ochre through shades of tan to purple. Sea stars nearly succumbed to a wasting disease in recent years, but today I see dozens huddled along the sides of rocks and

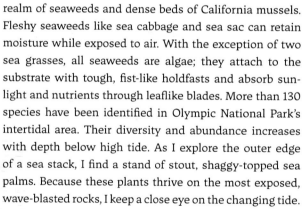

LEFT **Colorful seaweeds decorate parts of the rocky intertidal zone at Shi Shi Beach in Olympic National Park.** ABOVE **A granular claw crab strikes a defensive pose on the Olympic coast.** OPPOSITE **By preying on mussels, common purple or ochre sea stars define the lower limits of California mussel beds, as seen here at Second Beach in Olympic National Park. Sea star populations were decimated in recent years by a climate-related wasting disease. With the exception of massive sunflower stars, they are now recovering.**

channels, grimly weathering the assault of fresh air. When the tide is in, sea stars are aggressive and adept predators. They can pry tough mussel shells apart as easily as you and I crack peanuts. Then, inserting their stomachs into the open shells, they digest their meal in place, but only during high tide. So they limit their range to the middle to lower reaches of the intertidal area. To escape predation, mussels congregate higher. By clearing the lower rocks of mussel beds, sea stars also increase intertidal diversity; a host of other organisms, barnacles, limpets, and seaweeds colonize newly cleared patches.

Heavy surf and wave-tossed logs also clear patches in densely populated intertidal communities, allowing early successional species to take hold. It's a curiously satisfying thought: the same forces that work, winter by winter, to dismantle this wild and rugged coast also grace it with beauty and natural abundance.

The lush gardens of the extreme low tide zone stay hidden beneath the waves this breezy afternoon, so I miss the multihued rainbow seaweeds, the dark olivine sugar kelps, the long waving fronds of alaria. Prehistoric-looking sea cucumbers also remain hidden, as do most of those skittish though well-armored coastal denizens, the crabs. The sudden swell of a wave through a large tide pool alerts me to the changing tide, and I begin picking my way back over kelp-slicked rocks to shore. A light rain starts as I reach the beach, and fresh tracks in wet sand tell me my friends have started back. I can see them a little ways up the beach. With luck (but no help from us), the beginnings of a bouillabaisse will be simmering in the stockpot back at one of our cabins in La Push.

Gulls settle quietly along a shallow creek where it riffles over beach stones. And a pair of eagles perches in a leaning spruce, their hooked beaks and white heads prominent against the clouds. It's an image both fierce and quiescent, like the seasonal moods of this wild coast, and one I'll keep with me through the rainy weeks to come. ❖

TOP **Green anemones line a tide pool at Second Beach in Olympic National Park.** BOTTOM RIGHT **An opalescent nudibranch and aggregating anemones shelter in a tide pool at Ruby Beach in Olympic National Park.** BOTTOM LEFT **Purple and red sea urchins populate a tide pool at Salt Creek County Park on the Strait of Juan de Fuca.** OPPOSITE **Going tide pooling at low tide on Rialto Beach in Olympic National Park**

TOP LEFT **A luminous alabaster nudibranch and rainbow seaweed in a tide pool along the Strait of Juan de Fuca.** TOP RIGHT **Bull kelp washes up on the beach along Freshwater Bay on the Strait of Juan de Fuca.** BOTTOM RIGHT **Hermit crabs tangle at Tongue Point Marine Life Sanctuary at Salt Creek on the Strait of Juan de Fuca.** OPPOSITE **A giant Pacific octopus crawls between pier pilings as a scuba diver looks on. Encounters with this huge, intelligent eight-armed cephalopod are one of the highlights of scuba diving in the Pacific Northwest.**

# Sea Otter Recovery

Fuzzy-faced, graceful swimmers, sea otters are among the most beloved denizens of the wild Olympic coast. Their presence once more in the nearshore is the result of reintroduction of otters from Alaska after the local population was decimated by overhunting.

The natural range of the sea otter, *Enhydra lutris*, includes the coastlines of Russia, Japan, and North America. Native people of the Olympic peninsula coexisted with sea otters, hunting them for food and their coats. Sea otters have no blubber and keep warm in cold ocean waters with their luxuriant double-layered, waterproof fur. They have the thickest pelage of any animal, with more than a million hairs per square inch.

The arrival in the mid-1700s of first hunters from Russia and then traders and explorers from North America resulted in the near extirpation of the local populations by 1900, with the animals' pelts shipped to distant markets, including China. The last known sea otter in Washington was shot in 1911.

Sea otters are a keystone species, meaning they are essential in terms of the plants and animals that live there, what food is available, and how a community of plants and animals functions. The loss of sea otters resulted in a loss of kelp because of the key role that otters play in regulating sea urchin populations. With no otters to eat the urchins, the grazers mowed down the seafloor vegetation, including kelp. Not for nothing are these bare spots on the seafloor called "urchin barrens."

Reintroduction began in 1969 with sea otters collected in Alaska. More sea otters were also moved to other sites in Alaska and British Columbia. With the return of the sea otter has come the rise of kelp forests offshore of the Olympic coast, providing a nursery for young salmon, rockfish, crab larvae, and more. The kelp also provides shelter for sea otters, who raft up in the kelp beds, adrift on the tide, winding their babies in the long blades for safekeeping at the surface as moms dive down for food.

More mammals are on the move back to their home territory in the Olympics. Fishers have also been reintroduced to Washington to rebuild their numbers. A member of the weasel family, *Pekania pennanti* is another animal that was trapped nearly to extinction for its lush pelt. Successful reintroductions to the Olympic Peninsula beginning in 2008 by the National Park Service, the Washington Department of Fish and Wildlife, and other partners including the Makah Tribe and the nonprofit Conservation Northwest have resulted in boosts to the local population that is now reproducing on its own.

About the size of a house cat, fishers feed on rodents, hares, and even porcupines. Fishers were extirpated from Washington by the 1930s due to over-trapping, poisoning, and loss of their forest habitat. The fishers reintroduced to the Olympic region, including the Elwha Valley and Ozette Lake areas, were brought from British Columbia.

With sea otters returned to the coast and fishers being restored to the forest, the suite of animal life in the Olympic region is that much more complete. Perhaps next will come the wolf, as this native carnivore gradually extends its range in Washington to recolonize the Olympics.

—Lynda V. Mapes

ABOVE **A sea otter floats with her pup in the waters off Tatoosh Island on the Makah Indian Reservation.** OPPOSITE **A sea otter and pup feast on crab. Northern sea otters have a range from Alaska down the coasts of British Columbia and Washington. An estimated 2,700 otters now make their home along the Washington coast.**

TOP Surfers take to the waves during a camp organized by Warm Current. The group is dedicated to leading surf camps for—and in partnership with—tribal nations along the Washington coast. BOTTOM A driftwood campfire at twilight warms a backpacker's camp on Second Beach in Olympic National Park. OPPOSITE Kayakers paddle calm, kelp-strewn waters of Freshwater Bay in a county park on the Strait of Juan de Fuca.

The peninsula's large lowland lakes were carved by ice age glaciers and are fed and freshened by Olympic rivers and streams. ABOVE Lake Quinault, known for its diverse fisheries, is nestled into the Quinault rain forest and is bordered by Olympic National Park and Olympic National Forest. It is managed by the Quinault Indian Nation and is the site of historic Lake Quinault Lodge. LEFT Lake Crescent graces the northern edge of Olympic National Park and hosts two fish species unique to the Olympics: Crescenti and Beardslee trout. The lake is home to historic Lake Crescent Lodge. The Spruce Railroad Trail, a popular hiking and biking route, traces the lake's northern shoreline.

Hundreds of subalpine lakes are scattered like jewels throughout the Olympic Mountains. Frozen and snow-covered for much of the year, they are magnets for backpackers in summer. High lakes are also critical habitats for native amphibians: salamanders, newts, frogs, and toads. To preserve and recover these populations, stocking of non-native fish was discontinued in Olympic National Park in the 1970s. The three lakes shown on the opposite page are all found in Seven Lakes Basin in the upper Sol Duc watershed. OPPOSITE TOP LEFT **Round Lake;** OPPOSITE TOP RIGHT **Heart Lake** OPPOSITE BOTTOM **Lunch Lake.**

A coastal Sitka spruce forest borders Cape Flattery on the Makah Indian Reservation.

# Qʷidičča?a·tx̌ (Qwih-dich-chuh-ahtX), or "People of the Cape"

*Maria Parker Pascua (Hita·?a·?oƛ), **Makah Tribe***

## The Makah Relationship to Our Waterways and Land

Why is this area so special to the Makah people? Rocky areas, the sea, and landscapes including the rain forests and our numerous waterways—they were all given to us by the One Above, the Daylight One who is the Supreme Being and Creator of this area. We are grateful we were placed here in this rich environment. The Creator of each new day gave our ancestors the knowledge, experience, and abilities to live in this area, navigate the sea, and sustain ourselves with its abundance.

Just like other culture groups and their respective languages, we too have several ways to express terms for how God is known to us. ƛisi·q̓?ak (kl'ih-seeq̓-uhk), or the "Daylight," is one of the words for God who blessed our people with the ability to be in oneness with our environment; our people prayed for their very breath of life, their health, and their abilities to sustain themselves. They asked for guidance and success to accomplish their endeavors.

We have songs for various occasions; some songs are prayer songs, while some are for or about the animals that provided for our nourishment. We have songs about land mammals, sea mammals, birds, and other beings known to us in our culture. The success of obtaining provisions in our area was attributed to help via prayer and spiritual preparedness, emotional stability in the endeavor, positive mental preparation, and constant physical practice of the method used to secure food or accomplish a goal. This inclusive procedure is called hi·dasubač (hee-duh-soo-buhch), or "traditional preparation." The One Above was thanked, and the creature giving its life was thanked and celebrated as in the following example of bringing in a whale after a successful hunt.

Songs welcomed the whale to the village; welcomed the returning hunters; praised the power that made it all possible. (Makah Tribal Council 1995, 3).

There was a definite respect for the One Above and a spiritual connection with our natural environment. We learned about our surroundings through prayer, observation, and communication with creatures and their habitats, as well as through visions, dreams, ancestral teachings, and direct experiences. Our environment permeates and inspires us. Even the smallest of things in nature can influence our lives: a spider makes a web to catch its food, while a fisherman makes nets to catch salmon. Whether on land or in the water, there are associations and connections between acts of creation.

The Makah Tribe is comprised of five permanent villages and numerous seasonal sites. Ozette, Tsooyes, and Wyaatch villages are located on the Pacific Ocean side; Deah and Bahaada villages are on the long saltwater or "strait" side. The village of Ozette borders Olympic National Park.

Some early documents refer to our tribe as the Claset ƛaˑʔasatx̌ (klah-uh-suhtX), meaning "Cape Dwellers" and "Outer Coast." Hilary Stewart clarifies this name in John Jewitt's narrative, referring to the Makah people as Kla-iz-arts or ƛaˑʔasatx̌. When we arrived at Friendly Cove or Yuquot on Vancouver Island to trade in the early 1800s, he wrote, "These people are not only very expert in whaling, but are great hunters of the sea otter and other animals with which their country is said to abound" (Stewart 1987, 97). Elk, beaver, and cougar hides were mentioned as items of trade, but we hunted many other animals, like black bear and smaller game, along with various types of birds. Our Makah Museum has over 55,000 artifacts; most range from three hundred to five hundred years old, but there are other items from sites in our area that are thousands of years old. Detailed information on Makah food sources can be found in *Ozette Archaeology Project Research Reports, Volume II: Fauna*, which also details faunal analysis; mammals, including land and sea mammals; fish subsistence; invertebrate (like octopus and shellfish) subsistence patterns; avifaunal or bird remains; and whale utilization at Ozette (Samuels 1994).

**Makah gillnet in the Sooes River on the Makah Indian Reservation**

## The Rain, the Water, the Salmon

According to tradition, other beings, land and sea creatures, trees, plants, and even what are referred to by others as "inanimate objects," like rocks, were considered to have some human characteristics. One of our legends says the Changer came and turned people into other things. In that way, the salmon are also known as the salmon people. They start their life in freshwater, then live in the salt chuck for a time. They know who they are and where they come from, and they return to their place of origin to reproduce their kind. They ensure the future of their offspring by sacrificing themselves so their progeny live on, encoded with locational knowledge and connected with the First Peoples of this area who honor their return.

Salmon is highly valued by our people. We fish all species of salmon along with other fish such as halibut, cod, flounder, sole, perch, herring, and smelt, to name a few. We cannot diminish the value we have for other seafoods such as crab, octopus, and all manner of shellfish—from clams, mussels, barnacles, gooseneck barnacles, and urchins on down to the periwinkle. But of all the types of seafoods, it is the salmon who come back from the ocean, traveling through land areas by way of rivers and streams, and we enjoy eating salmon in all stages, from salmon eggs to ocean-caught salmon to freshwater salmon upon their return.

Rain too, connects with saltwater, falling on both land and sea. The creatures inhabiting our land and ocean are affected by the freshwater in their respective areas. Also, rain can cause movement in the schools of fish such as the salmon. But rain or shine, cloud or fog, wind or calm, our people find the salmon; long ago we followed their routes by triangulating landmarks to obtain this wonderful food source.

Our smokehouses to this day fill up with fish that still sustain our people. Our tribal government is active with our fish hatchery and fisheries department and advocates for the protection and continuation of our fish stocks. The blueback, or sockeye, on Ozette Lake is also monitored by our tribe in efforts to restock the fish runs damaged by logging and the aggressive depletion of this stock.

All in all, we must continue to protect salmon as a food source, but this food source is not just limited to the people. Salmon are also important to the wolves of the sea—our orcas, who hunt in their ocean pods just as wolf packs do on land. Our people, both Makah and Nuu-chah-nulth, like the orcas, are fishers of salmon and hunters of seal, sea lion, and whale. But for the kawad (kuh-wuhd), or "killer whale," some pods are particularly salmon eaters. There are various other animals whose subsistence includes salmon, and they partake of salmon in all of its life stages. The food chain includes more than us, and salmon are so important for the survival of other living creatures in the intricate balance of life.

## Rain Forest and Cedar

We live in a rain forest climate with drenching rain at times from fall until spring and occasional heavy winter storms. Our people are used to these weather patterns. Water is considered sacred and is, of course, necessary to our existence. Our elder Makah speakers told of the cultural practice of stopping to pray when encountering a stream along their way. They took water from the stream into their mouth and, while holding it in their mouth for a moment, they communicated with God from their spirit, giving thanks for fresh water and making other supplication known only by the individual and the One Above. Then they would expel the water by spraying it from the mouth, sending the prayer out to travel in a sprinkling of directions to be heard and answered.

Our people had a daily intentional practice of bathing and praying at daybreak at select water sources, many of which were located in our beautiful forested area; water for bathing, cedar sprigs for scrubbing, along with prayer was a sacred practice to us. We associated cleansing the outer body with a spiritual cleansing of our inner soul to start each new day. Sometimes forms of abstinence were also adhered to like fasting. In a humble way, we asked the One Above for assistance in tasks, abilities, or aid in our endeavors.

We are thankful for where we live. Our rain forests are important, and the constant rain feeds the greenery, making our area such a beautiful place to reside. Though we live different lifestyles today, it is still important to identify and respect all the trees, plants, and their biomes.

When logging occurs and reforestation is based on what type of timber sells best, it ignores the environment that first existed in that space. What trees and vegetation grow best together naturally? How can we preserve plants that would normally grow in this space? What about edible or medicinal plants, or plants used to make functional objects? Knowledge of the land areas such as marshes, caves, hills, mountains, and prairies, along with the plant and animal life using these areas, is crucial. We appreciate our tribe's foresight in setting aside old-growth acreage on our reservation for the generations to come; in that regard, we have like goals, as Olympic National Park also enacts a protection of place by preserving the park's natural environment, including its trees, for the future.

Every tree has its importance, but cedar is one of the most versatile trees used by our people. The inner bark is separated and used to make baskets, string, rope, and clothing. The roots and limbs are peeled and cut for use in making pack baskets and clam baskets, heavy rope and wythes. The wood can make longhouses, canoes, boxes, benches, poles, paddles, masks, and other carvings. Limbs and sprigs are used in a sacred manner in ceremony, cleansing, and protection. Cedar was of precious value to our ancestors as it was so versatile, providing clothing, hats, baskets, rope and twine, canoes for transportation, longhouses for shelter . . . it is no wonder it was considered sacred. After all, life is sacred, and the cedar truly met so many of our basic needs. We are so pleased that our Makah cedar carving and weaving traditions carry on to this day.

Trees, bushes, and plants have their own life cycles, and when they die, they dry and wither. But when they are used by First Peoples, some are transformed into something else—for example, making the cedar into a canoe, giving it another life connected with the people who will use it as transportation. Canoes are respected and appreciated, carrying people to destinations where they can

**Sunset light in May at Hobuck Beach on the Makah Indian Reservation**

obtain food, visit others, or share in cultural celebrations. And recycling was common. A carver may pray while harvesting cedar, thankful for the tree; they pray with intent for what it will become and how valuable it is to the people. The wood might become a longhouse board, but eventually it wears out, so the carver may repurpose it to make a necessary patch for a canoe crack. That piece of wood then lives on as part of the canoe, keeping the people safe from a leak in the vessel. Thriftiness and repurposing gave such items yet another way to live life with the people who asked for the materials' unique assistance and enabled the item's transformation or augmentation to exist in a variety of forms for a variety of reasons.

## Rock Relevance

Our largest island is Tatoosh Island, referred to as the "stone house" by some Makah elders. Though it has margins of beach area as well as vegetation on its top, its base is rock. Sea caves cut back into the island, and other sea rocks are located near its perimeter. We had a village on this island; it was a strategic lookout close to fishing, sealing, and whaling locations.

Some of the rocks in our area convey information even today by way of our oldest art form, the rock carvings our ancestors made by way of their petroglyphs. One of our oldest art forms is the petroglyph, many of which are carved into the rocks. These are images our ancestors left. Some images represent people, like a fisherman spearing fish or depictions of both men and women. There are whale petroglyphs marking the livelihoods of our largest food source. Other animals and beings are also portrayed. Some of the images can be found further along our territory (meaning our territory before Olympic National Park's creation and before the reservation land reduction), which is extensive.

We did not think of just our land area as territory; our waterways went out to the blue waters for fur seal hunting and out to Forty Mile Bank or La Perouse for one of our halibut fishing areas. We have Makah place names down to Cape Johnson on our ocean side and to Lyre River and Freshwater Bay areas along the long saltwater strait side. We use an inland division from that southernmost point to the easternmost point for hunting land mammals and birds and gathering materials, medicine, and food. Around these various areas, there are numerous outlying sea rocks, sea caves, beach and river rocks, interior rocks, and black granite, to name a few.

Our sea rocks are home to many of our seafood resources and sea mammals. Sea caves were not only used by seals and sea lions, however; in ancient times some caves were considered sacred sites, others were sealand sea lion caves.

Rocks were essential for so many things: small pebbles were used in boys' slingshots, teaching aim and coordination. River rocks were used to heat and cook food. Heavy rocks were used to hold down roofboards on longhouses. Cannonball-sized rocks were used in war canoes for sea battles or hurled down from higher elevations onto enemies on land or sea.

Black granite was strong and thus used to make mauls for splitting wood, but when left in its natural smooth form, it can also be used for pounding bark or flattening design work in a basket. Quartz was strong, too, and used to make precision points for sharp tools; it also has significance in certain ceremonies.

In our stories, all terrain and marine areas held items and life forms that had spiritual significance to us. We perceived rock to have a life and a life force created by the One Above.

It was made with purpose, and humans create even more from it, designing more purposes for the stone like fishing sinkers, useful tools, and weapons. All things, no matter how small, need our respect and thankfulness for just being.

## Conclusion

Salmon, cedar, rock, and rain are key components of Olympic National Park, but they have an even older history with the First Peoples of this area. We live in and with these cherished treasures of life and nature, God-given, bountiful, and beautiful.

Our social system includes chiefs or head people and leaders tasked with the responsibility to care for their people and place; some hold stations to carry out functions or lead activities for their families, extended families, or the entire tribe. In our times today, our Makah Tribal Council are elected leaders tasked with governing our people and our land and waterways. We are part of a whole, and each one of us is important. Each of us can make a difference by instilling care for what we must maintain today for future generations to come. There is a Makah teaching about reciprocity, and fortunately this teaching is passed down and unfolds today through the sharing of food, workload, and care. May our teachings continue, our tribe thrive, and our environment both here and in the park remain.

LEFT **Rugged Cape Flattery at the northwest tip of the Olympic Peninsula is also the northwesternmost point in the contiguous United States. Homeland of the Makah Tribe for thousands of years, the Cape can be reached by a short trail.** OPPOSITE **A whale carving on an interpretive display post greets winter hikers at the Shi Shi Beach trailhead on the Makah Indian Reservation.**

# Currents of Conservation

Not far inland from the mouth of the Elwha River is the Elwha Klallam people's creation site. For nearly a century, "Coiled Basket" rock, the place where the Creator bathed and blessed the first people, was inundated behind the Elwha Dam. In 2012, dam removal returned it once more to the light. When Elwha Klallam people visited the sacred site that summer, tribal chair Frances Charles described the experience as overwhelming. "You could feel the power of the rock," she said. "Everything is coming back to life." Upriver, the site of an ancient Elwha village emerged from a second reservoir. It dates back more than eight thousand years. When contrasted with the few brief centuries since Europeans first encountered the Olympic Peninsula, dates like this stagger the imagination; eight thousand years ago, farming was just taking hold in Europe. Yet people were here, mastering ways to live within the diverse and ever-changing natural systems of this land, and passing the knowledge on to generations that followed.

The long and ever-deepening story of human presence on the peninsula is one of endurance, ingenuity, and vision. Mastodon and bison grazed the open, post-Pleistocene landscape when the earliest people left evidence of their

BELOW Vine maple leaves display autumn colors by a western redcedar in Olympic National Park. OPPOSITE Garry oaks, native to Sequim Prairie, were a major food source for both Native people and a number of wildlife species. Prairies were regularly burned and managed by indigenous people. Since 2003, volunteers have planted and nurtured some 1,500 oak seedlings north of Carrie Blake Park in Sequim of to help restore this valuable habitat.

presence. A band of hunters butchered a mastodon on the shore of a glacial pond near the present town of Sequim. Organic material that accompanied a few stone and bone artifacts discovered at the site was dated at 13,800 years ago.

The peninsula's climate has fluctuated radically since the last ice age. Sea levels rose and fell; prairies and wetlands spread and diminished over lowland plains. Warming periods brought extensive wildfires. The "Little Ice Age" pushed alpine glaciers once more into lowland valleys. Eventually, the mixed conifer forests we know today came to dominate the landscape. Throughout that time, people adapted to and shaped emerging ecosystems in significant ways. A deeply rooted sense of connection emerged with the land. Mountain hunters following elk and deer trails between four thousand and eight thousand years ago left evidence of their presence at places like Slab Camp, Hurricane Ridge, and Seven Lakes Basin. Coastal village sites at Wa'atch, Ozette, Hoko River, and Tse-whit-zen in Port Angeles reveal complex and sophisticated cultures that mastered ocean fishing, sea mammal hunting, and whaling as far back as four thousand years ago.

What we think of today as conservation and care for the land and its creatures ran like a current through the peninsula's watersheds for millennia. Native people were the original stewards of this land, and Indigenous practices shaped the nature of the landscape. Prairie burning prevented incursion by forests and enhanced browse for game. The cultivation of camas and other food plants fostered botanical diversity and influenced the ecology of prairies. Tending berry grounds and oak groves enhanced habitats for wildlife. Salmon fishing in home rivers allowed management of individual stocks (a practice recognized today as far more sustainable than mixed-stock ocean fishing), and first salmon ceremonies insured that portions of salmon runs passed upstream to spawn. Centuries-old shell middens at coastal village sites testify to sustainable shellfish harvesting; bird and sea mammal bones in the middens confirm stable hunting practices. Cultures and ecosystems coevolved fluidly.

Though fundamentally different in nature and purpose, early European conservation currents on the peninsula can be seen as flowing from this river of long-term stewardship. By the last years of the nineteenth century, history had finally caught up with the Olympic Peninsula, and industrial resource destruction was reaching its peak. Extensive clearcuts fed trees to hungry sawmills that spewed waste into rivers and bays. Commercial canneries consumed wild salmon runs. Even the once-abundant Olympic elk were being slaughtered to supply meat to logging camps and burgeoning towns; their eye teeth were marketed as watch fobs to members of the Elks Lodge.

Long-resilient ecosystems of the peninsula were suddenly faced with irreparable harm.

At the national level, conservationists called on representatives in Congress to halt wholesale forest destruction and preserve some of our last great western forests. In response, an 1891 law granted the president power to create forest reserves. Six years later, President Cleveland established the Olympic Forest Reserve. It encompassed more than 2.1 million acres, nearly a third of the peninsula, and included the heavily forested western slope as far as the Pacific shore. It was largest of federal reserves at the time and, harboring some sixty billion board feet of

choice timber, clearly the most commercially valuable. Its creation was a bold and visionary move for its day, but it proved tragically short-lived. A few years later, President McKinley slashed it by nearly a quarter million acres, consigning some of the most outstanding ancient forests in the nation to logging.

Around that time another current was gathering momentum. Two Olympic Mountain explorers, Lieutenant Joseph O'Neil and James Wickersham, independently proposed a national park for the Olympics. Thus began a struggle over the fate of Olympic forest lands that would dominate the next half century. Conservationists brought their cause to a nationwide audience, and two national leaders rose to play key roles in the protection of Olympic wildlands. One was a rough-and-tumble adventurer, war hero, big-game hunter, and naturalist; the other, his distant cousin, was an urbane progressive and reformer who was moved to take a personal interest in the lands that would become Olympic National Park.

President Theodore Roosevelt responded to a public outcry over the plundering of Olympic elk by using the Antiquities Act to create the Mount Olympus National Monument in 1909. The monument protected a core of interior habitat, setting the elk that would later bear his name on a path to

Olympic National Park protects the full range of peninsula forest types from coastal Sitka spruce-hemlock forests to these lichen-bedecked mountain forests along Hurricane Ridge Road.

recovery. It failed to include lowland valleys, however, and organizations like The Mountaineers began to lobby for a larger national park. Roosevelt had earlier placed the Olympic Forest Reserve under the US Department of Agriculture to be managed for sustained yield and redesignated it as Olympic National Forest. Responding to concerns over the commercial hunting of seabirds for their feathers, he also created the Washington Islands National Wildlife Refuges, protecting some of the most productive seabird nesting habitats on the Pacific coast. By the time he left office in 1909, Theodore Roosevelt had left a generous legacy of federally protected lands on the peninsula: a national forest, a national monument, and national wildlife refuges. Broad in geography and scale, they became the central structures for protecting the remarkable Olympic ecosystem. The currents of conservation had merged into a river.

Shifting political winds then as now shape federal land policies. By the time Franklin Delano Roosevelt entered the White House in 1933, severe national monument reductions of up to a third the total acreage coupled with accelerated cutting on Olympic National Forest—from twelve

million board feet in 1920 to 175 million by the end of the decade—sparked renewed calls for a national park. The park movement coalesced into a national cause, and three citizen advocates emerged to help make the park a reality: Irving Brant, an influential St. Lewis newspaper columnist; Willard Van Name, an ecologically minded scientist with the Museum of Natural History; and Rosalie Edge, a fiery former suffragette and Audubon activist who had dedicated herself to environmental causes. Edge visited the peninsula on a tour of western parks in the mid-1930s and became an outspoken advocate for Olympic National Park. Her Emergency Conservation Committee published articles and mailed thousands of pamphlets arguing for preservation of the Olympics' unmatched temperate rain forests. The campaign attracted the support of conservation organizations, outdoor clubs, scientific societies, and natural history museums across the country. Importantly, it caught the attention of President Roosevelt. He toured the peninsula in 1937 and was met by thousands of schoolchildren who gathered in Port Angeles to show support for a national park. With FDR's leadership, US Forest Service

and timber industry opposition to a large park was overcome, and the following year he signed the bill creating Olympic National Park. The new park included extensive lowland rain forest valleys and allowed for additions of generous corridors along the Queets River and wild Pacific coast. Olympic was conceived as a wilderness park that embraced critical ecosystem components. Watersheds, winter elk ranges, salmon spawning and rearing habitats, and biologically productive lowland forests were included. This scientifically informed vision, made clear in legislative language, bequeathed to all Americans one of the richest and most significant ecological preserves on the planet.

No sooner was it established, however, than the park had to be defended from efforts to strip away its rain forest valleys and construct a highway along its wilderness coast. As it happened, another woman conservation leader rose to defend the park's forests and wild coastline. Polly Dyer moved to the Pacific Northwest in 1950.

She helped found the Northwest chapter of the Sierra Club and worked with The Mountaineers and other organizations to protect Northwest wildlands. She soon found herself deep in a campaign to defend the Olympic rain forest, and in 1958 she organized a group hike led by US Supreme Court Justice William O. Douglas that scuttled plans for a coast highway. Dyer led successful campaigns to defend the Quinault rain forest, add Shi Shi Beach and Point of the Arches to the park in the 1970s, and protect nearly ninety thousand acres as wilderness in Olympic National Forest as well as designate 95 percent of Olympic National Park as wilderness in the following decade.

I was in my early twenties when Polly Dyer introduced me to the cause of conservation in the Olympics. She was an inspiring example, and a half century later I still work with Olympic Park Advocates, the citizens' group she led so effectively, to defend the park and promote wildlands protection on the Olympic Peninsula. ❖

ABOVE **Felling an old-growth western redcedar**
OPPOSITE **Selective cutting leaves standing trees for habitat and future snag development on Washington Department of Natural Resources land in the lower Sol Duc Valley.**

## Women Take the Lead

For nearly a century, women have been at the forefront of major campaigns to protect Olympic wild country, often taking on male-dominated industries like timber and highway construction. I checked in with my friend and conservation ally Connie Gallant, who had made a study of women conservation heroes of the Olympics, for a fuller story.

Connie is herself a respected Olympic conservation leader. Arriving in the United States from her native Cuba at thirteen and speaking no English, she later made her way west and settled with her husband on the Olympic Peninsula in the early 1980s. When the US Forest Service released plans to log scenic Mount Walker, Connie educated herself in forest issues. Since then she has guided the Olympic Forest Coalition in its efforts to protect forests, streams, and endangered species in her adopted home. She also serves as chair of the Wild Olympics Campaign, a popular effort that champions legislation to designate 126,000 acres of new wilderness in Olympic National Forest and create nineteen National Wild and Scenic Rivers on the peninsula. Connie speaks with experience about the role women have played in Olympic conservation.

"Rosalie [Edge] and Polly [Dyer] were a generation apart, but both came from a time when women were expected to stay in the background and keep their ideas to themselves," Connie told me. "However, when they spoke out knowledgably and passionately on behalf of the environment, people took notice." Connie reminded me Rosalie was a national leader in bird conservation, and Polly worked for the passage of the 1964 Wilderness Act as well as the creation of Glacier Peak Wilderness and North Cascades National Park. She mentioned some other powerful women who moved conservation forward on the peninsula. "Eleanor Stopps and Lorna Smith worked tirelessly to create the Protection Island National Wildlife Refuge, home to 70 percent of nesting seabirds of Puget Sound," she said. "Norma Turner led the effort that stopped an industrial oil port from being built west of Port Angeles, and Bonnie Phillips became a champion of old-growth forests in Washington, speaking out on

behalf of threatened northern spotted owls and marbled murrelets, both put at risk by clearcutting." Connie told me that Bonnie was struck by a strain of rheumatism that kept her mostly confined to a wheelchair, yet she still organized for forest protections that eventually led to the Northwest Forest Plan and the Roadless Rule that prohibited road building and development in fifty-eight million acres of national forest lands, including more than eighty-five thousand acres in the Olympic National Forest.

"That tradition continues, and there are more women than I could mention," Connie mused. "But when I read about the increasing numbers of salmon making their way up the Elwha River, I think of Elwha tribal chair Frances Charles and the incredible vision and leadership she provided to see the Elwha dams removed and salmon restored to the river." She reflected for a moment. "Women pioneers have been celebrated on the peninsula, but women conservation leaders—that's a story that's yet to be fully told."

In recent years, Connie has been working with the Olympic Forest Collaborative, a cooperating group of leaders and representatives from the environmental community, timber industry, and federal and local governments who are working together to increase timber volume from Olympic National Forest while benefiting watersheds, forest health, and the peninsula's rural economy. Ecological restoration has become a dominant theme in Olympic conservation. But a larger threat overshadows conservation efforts today and is forcing scientists, land managers, and conservationists to think in new ways about maintaining the integrity of the Olympic ecosystem.

—Tim McNulty

ABOVE **Connie Gallant is chair of the Wild Olympics Campaign and one of a long line of women environmental activists on the peninsula.** OPPOSITE **Thanks to the work of activists, Point of the Arches and Shi Shi Beach along the northern coast were added to Olympic National Park in 1976. Shi Shi is now among the most popular wilderness beaches in the park.**

THIS PAGE **Park scientists survey pollinators in the former Lake Aldwell reservoir site following removal of the Elwha dams.** OPPOSITE **The University of Washington's Dr. James Freund conducts canopy research in an old-growth Douglas-fir in Olympic National Park.**

Surf is bathed in golden light looking west from ʔéʔɬx̣ʷaʔ cáwŋən (Elwha Beach) on the Lower Elwha Klallam Reservation.

# Language Revitalization

*Wendy Sampson, Lower Elwha Klallam Tribe*

## Indigenous Place Names

A cloud of dust rises as I pull my van into a gravel patch on the side of the road. I greet the land and plants in my Indigenous Klallam language: "ʔə́y' skʷáči nesčáyəʔčaʔ. mán' cn ʔuʔ ʔə́yəs cn ʔaʔ či nəstáči" ("Good day my friends and relatives. I'm very happy to arrive here"). My children join me, buckets in hand, ready to walk the forest trails in search of berries. I brought them to gather traditional foods, but they will also learn the history of the area, the traditional Klallam place names, and how to speak to the land respectfully in the Klallam language.

As Indigenous peoples of the Olympic Peninsula, some of the ways we can maintain our traditions are by visiting ancestral places, carrying on traditional activities, and using our Klallam language. When we visit a site traditionally used by our ancestors, we are not only standing in the present but also visiting the past. We remember the people who once walked along the same beaches, rivers, and alpine trails. We think of our grandmothers and grandfathers who once looked upon the same mountain and ocean views, who once practiced the same activities at the same places, uttered the same words in the Klallam language, and spoke to the land in the same way. When we use our traditional place names, or sing a traditional song, we are connecting with the people who came before us and letting the land know that we are the descendants of the ones who once lived here and that we belong to this land. Though access to many traditional places is now prohibited due to privatization of the land—and the number of people who practice traditional activities and use traditional place names has been reduced due to cultural assimilation and language loss—there is still a strong connection between the land and its people. In this essay I will share a brief history of the Klallam people and examine the role that their Indigenous language plays in their ongoing relationship with the land. I will illustrate how Klallam people today can maintain their connection to the land and their ancestors while passing on traditional knowledge to the next generation by reviving the Klallam language, using traditional place names, and carrying on traditional practices in their ancestral places.

Since time immemorial, the nəxʷsƛ̕ay̕əm̕ (Klallam people) lived in many permanent and seasonal villages along the shorelines of the Salish Sea and up rivers and streams into the foothills of the Olympic Mountains. They hunted, fished, and gathered from the saltwater up to the headwaters of the rivers travelling into and over the mountains. Klallam culture flourished for innumerable generations until rapid changes occurred; diseases brought by European explorers in the late 1700s decimated Klallam populations, then settlers began claiming ownership of the land in the 1800s. The Klallam struggled to survive during this time as they were unable to obtain food in their traditional ways because of restricted access to traditional sites. Even though they secured the "right of taking fish at usual and accustomed grounds and stations" and the right to hunt and gather "on open and unclaimed lands" when they signed the Point No Point Treaty of 1855, struggles intensified when the State of Washington imposed laws requiring fishing licenses in 1910. At that time Indigenous people were not considered citizens and hence it was illegal for them to fish, and elders recalled people being jailed for taking fish—even spawned out salmon. Displacement from their home sites, lack of access to traditional areas, prohibition of subsistence activities, and a changing socioeconomic climate forced many Klallam to adapt to a new way of life. On the Elwha, some families were able to claim land under the Indian Homestead Act of 1884 and became farmers; others became loggers or seasonal laborers. Several Klallam families tried to maintain a traditional Coast-Salish lifestyle, living off the land and water, by moving to rocky shores west of the Elwha River and beaches at Ediz Hook. No matter how families maintained their livelihood, all Klallam children were required to attend government-run Indian boarding schools or day-schools and learn the English language. Late tribal elders shared stories of being punished when caught speaking Klallam. It was during this time that traditional practices, language, and history faded as assimilation efforts

increased. Thankfully, not all traditional knowledge disappeared. Some information has slipped through the cracks of colonization and is still passed on to this day.

Like most Indigenous languages, Klallam was not a written language, however, and written documentation have preserved much of the language and the knowledge therein. The first person to write down Klallam words was Paul Kane, who travelled from Victoria to the Klallam village of ʔiʔíʔnəs (Ennis Creek), located in present-day Port Angeles, in 1847. Through the years Indian agents, missionaries, historians, linguists, cultural ethnologists, musicologists, anthropologists, and tribal members have documented the language and history of the elders (Montler 2015). This knowledge has been preserved by recording place names, traditional legends, personal anecdotes, songs, useful phrases, and detailed grammatical explanations provided in the Klallam dictionary and grammar books. All have greatly aided today's tribal cultural and linguistic revitalization efforts. This work started due to a surge of interest in studying Indigenous people and continued because people knew that the remaining elders were crucial to passing on information for the future. The elders who worked tirelessly being recorded and the caring people documenting their knowledge have given a precious gift to the world.

The documentation that has preserved linguistic, historical, and cultural knowledge has proven to be invaluable, especially the traditional place names and history. Knowing the names of places and how they were used before contact with Europeans provides evidence of continuous occupation of these areas and proves an ongoing cultural heritage, which are criteria the US government uses to determine a tribe's eligibility for federal recognition. This continuous occupation and use can also assist some tribes in disputes involving land ownership and traditional use areas where they exercise their treaty rights. Such was the case in the court case that led to the 1974 Boldt Decision reaffirming Washington state tribal rights to 50 percent of the harvestable fish. Detailed information regarding how and where the Klallam people gathered flora and fauna was presented by anthropologist

The Olympic hot springs are sacred to the Klallam people and are traditionally used for bathing, to cleanse oneself physically and spiritually.

Dr. Barbara Lane. Lane's well-documented reports about traditional places and uses ensured the Klallam would have access to their usual and accustomed areas for generations to come. But issues regarding governments and territory are not the only reason traditional place names and their historic uses are important.

Documentation of Klallam place names is also important because the structure of the words themselves can be used to look into the past. A place name can tell a story of the land and people. For example, according to linguist, Dr. Timothy Montler, who has documented the Klallam language for over twenty-five years, the village name "ʔiʔínəs" literally means "good chest." The -ínəs ("chest") suffix is metaphorically used for a headland because like a chest or breast a headland protrudes from the land. Dr. Montler says, "This name tells us how important that site was—both as a shelter and as a lookout vantage point to protect the entire harbor." He also notes that the Klallam place name for the inner Port Angeles Harbor, číxʷícən, means "enter back behind" and that this name "tells how the village was protected from the sea, weather, and invaders" (Montler, personal communication, 2022). The Klallam name for Sequim, sxʷčkʷíyəŋ, also has a story to tell. The meaning of this word is "a place to shoot," generally translated as "hunting grounds," relating to the rolling hills that overlook wide open prairies that once swarmed with elk. Another name of interest was documented by anthropologist Jacilee Wray in a report for the Olympic National Park. It is not a village name, but the name for the mountain range now called the Olympic Mountains. Tribal elders from both sides of the Strait of Juan de Fuca called them the sʎ́áy̓əməɬ x̣əy̓kʷəy̓éʔč, meaning "Klallam Mountains" (Wray 1997). With an understanding of the words and stories that go with the land, the Klallam people today

In 2019, this popular downtown Port Angeles park was renamed Pebble Beach Park—sŋaʔŋáʔant cáwŋən ʔəssaqɬúŋt—to honor the Lower Elwha Klallam people and acknowledge their long relationship with this land.

can connect not only with the land around them but also with their ancestors and the heritage of these places.

There are many examples of how language is helping Klallam people maintain their connections with the land, as well as their heritage and culture. In 2012 a group of Elwha Klallam youth hikers followed ancient paths over the Olympic Mountains, using Klallam names for places along the way that held special significance for hunting, gathering, and ceremonial activities. More groups of Klallam youth have completed this hike multiple times since then, as well as other hikes in the Olympics, reestablishing important connections between Klallam people and the land of their ancestors. In 2016 the City of Port Angeles worked in partnership with the LEKT language program to install street signs at a busy downtown intersection that had both English and Klallam words, honoring the connection the Klallam people have with that area. In 2019 tribal members successfully petitioned the City to rename the nearby park, which is now called sŋaʔŋáʔant cáwŋən ʔəssaqɫúŋt (Pebble Beach Park). Two beaches within the park also received Klallam names relating to the use of those traditional areas: sxʷtxʷás (to beach a canoe) and sxʷtčcéʔnəŋ̓ (to walk along the edge of the water on the beach). In 2022, areas that were once underwater behind the former dams on the Elwha River and shorelines that are being revived by sediment flowing from the mountains to the beaches are being renamed in the language as Klallam people are once again able to access and use these areas. These new place names, just like traditional place names, help connect Klallam people to the land they belong to and will continue to empower Klallam people to learn their language and ancestral ways.

Today many Klallam people like myself are working harder than ever to revive the Klallam language and perpetuate traditions by expanding language use and continuing ancestral practices in our traditional places. I started learning the Klallam language as a teenager, and began speaking to my own children in the language while they were still in my womb. I now teach the Klallam language to not only my own children, but also teenagers in the public school system in Port Angeles. In both my

Salmonberry bushes favor streamsides and bogs. Bright reddish-purple flowers yield to yellow-orange berries in early summer.

home and my classes we learn the language, the meaning of each part of each word, and the history and ways of the nəxʷsʎáy̓əm̓ (Klallam people). We learn about the relationship the Klallam people have always had with this land and that language used to speak to it. We learn about reciprocity and respect when gathering traditional foods. We learn about the ongoing efforts to protect the environment and sacred sites still used today. We drive down dirt roads, and walk the beaches and forests, with our buckets in hand. We carry the knowledge that has been given to us with good minds and hearts.

The Klallam people have lived here, taken care of this land, and passed on knowledge embedded in the language since time immemorial. As we look ahead we must continue that work by maintaining a connection to the land by continuing our traditional practices. We must be thankful for the gifts given to us by the land and those who came before us as we continue growing and using our language and ceremonies so that the information and ways of our ancestors will be carried on for generations to come.

# First Foods

It is the original diversified economy, with riches in every season: a web of life that feeds the Olympic Peninsula's First People year-round from an abundant land and sea. Called "First Foods," these were the staples Native people of the peninsula always relied on—and still do today. Hunting, fishing, and gathering rights to these foods and medicines—life sources, not just resources—were reserved by the First Peoples in treaties that Olympic Peninsula tribes signed with the United States in 1855. The treaties were a codification of the unwritten laws that sustain a way of life based on gifts from the Creator and a reciprocal relationship with nature that still abides.

That's why when COVID-19 first struck the area in 2020, the Makah Tribe knew just what to do. While communities beyond their borders sweated supply chains and scarcity, people at the Makah Reservation knew Washburn's General Store, the one grocery in Neah Bay, was just the beginning of how they would sustain themselves during a long COVID-19 lockdown. The tribe closed its borders to the outside world for more than two years to protect its people. Timothy J. Greene, Sr., chairman of the Makah Tribe, said the closure was supported by the community—which has no hospital and was unwilling to lose a single elder to the pandemic.

As the months of the lockdown turned into years, tribal members turned to one another, their skills, the land, and the sea. "It was a good reminder that we can be self-sustaining here for quite a while, as long as that ocean is healthy and we could get to that ocean and fishing grounds," Greene said.

The tribe also has a commercial grade meat grinder, vacuum sealer, canners, coolers, and freezers for community use. Chazley Brown, a coordinator of the Makah Food Security Program, offered classes in everything from fileting halibut to processing deer. Kippering, canning, smoking, drying, preserving, butchering: at home, hers is a kitchen of verbs. "All around, I don't think there's anything I can't help teach or show somebody," Brown said. "I try my best to do it all so we don't have to go to the store."

Meanwhile, the Jamestown S'Klallam Tribe has embraced a First Foods program to offer instruction, share recipes, and provide facilities for growing and processing traditional foods. "It is not that we are not depending on the food options that everyone uses today, but we are starting to lean more on the traditional foods, Indigenous foods that are healthier," said W. Ron Allen, chairman and CEO of the Jamestown S'Klallam Tribe. "It is a big deal to us; it's ingrained in everything we are doing. It's just obvious—these traditional foods provide the right kind of nutrients that everybody needs to be healthy. It is what our body is asking for. Not the processed foods." The tribe is offering workshops and field forays to gather everything from camas to shellfish and berries.

To Russell Hepfer, vice chairman of the Lower Elwha Klallam Tribe, one of the most delicious meals is smoked and dried fish, served with boiled potatoes—and seal oil for dipping. Urchins, smelt, berries, deer, and more are also favorites in the community. "All of the processed food and chemicals, it gets you fat and your body can't process it," Hepfer said. "Whereas the traditional food, it is good for you and good for your soul."

Mark Colson, an enrolled member of the Confederated Tribes of the Chehalis Reservation, agreed. "When you put these traditional

foods in your body, it heals you," he said. "It is the whole process of being really connected to our lands and our foods." He started gathering berries with his elders from an early age, and today berries remain a favorite food. Now his daughter is canning berries, too. "That makes me so proud," Colson said. "Everywhere we go we are always gathering, constantly learning, being fully aware of what the plants are doing, the way the plants grow. It is all connected, the language and all the rest of it."

Kris Miller of the Skokomish Tribe also looks to the plants in her homeland for weaving cedar bark, which she learned from her uncle Subiyay (Bruce Miller). Miller said she has been weaving cedar since she was about seven years old, learning how to gather sweetgrass and cattail for weaving along the way. Today she is the one teaching, and her hands are always busy. "What I think about is the future, when I am gone—are people going to know what I know? I want to make sure the culture is still living. The same with the foods and the medicine and the weaving, I am going to carry it on," she says. "It is to me important; it is our identity from the beginning of time, and our wealth. It is who we are. When I gather I think about our ancestors. How did they do this? Did they sit in this exact same place? When I go outside I see the importance of every little thing. And I am thankful for all of it."

ABOVE **The late Arlene DelaCruz roasts blueback salmon on cedar splits for the Olympic Coast National Marine Sanctuary dedication at Kalaloch.** OPPOSITE **One of the earliest wild berries to ripen, salmonberries are a prized First Food. Found in lowlands throughout the Olympic Peninsula, the salmon-colored berries are enjoyed fresh, mixed with salmon and salmon eggs, made into jam, or dried.**

At the Quinault Reservation on the outer coast of the peninsula, Tyson Johnson carries on the fishing tradition in his family that stretches back for generations. "We are connected to the sea; that is a really important connection that has been in our family since all the way back," Johnson said. In the summer of 2022, his family celebrated a season of abundance, with blueback sockeye, unique to the Quinault River system, returning in the biggest numbers since 1975. "It is such a blessing to see it come back like that; it is a reawakening of things I have not felt in a long time, the act of taking pride in harvesting, to see the health and vitality," Johnson said.

The community held a ceremony to bless and share the fish they believe comes from the same place in the ocean as they do. "We have a common tie. Having the ability to take care of them and to have them be part of our nutrition and abundance and to provide for the people is really special," Johnson said. "As stewards, we feel like we are doing what we are meant to do as part of our original instructions from the Creator."

—**Lynda V. Mapes**

**Blueback or Quinault salmon is a kind of sockeye salmon unique to the Quinault River; traditionally it is one of the most important salmon of the Quinault people. A major restoration project on the river above Lake Quinault is attempting to restore lost habitat for bluebacks.**

Shoreline alders are reflected in the calm waters of Lake Quinault. This glacial-carved lake, owned by the Quinault Indian Nation, is surrounded by spectacular temperate rain forest.

# Island in the Storm

With more than a million acres of protected lands, it would seem that the future health and viability of the Olympic ecosystem is assured. Olympic National Park alone protects 922,650 acres of the heart of the peninsula and along its Pacific coast. More than 95 percent of the park is designated as the Daniel J. Evans Wilderness. Five areas of Olympic National Forest adjoining the park, a total of 88,265 acres, are also wilderness. According to the 1964 Wilderness Act, these are lands "where the earth and its community of life are untrammeled by man, where man himself is a visitor who does not remain." The benefits of wilderness extend well beyond protected forests and fish and wildlife habitats; clean air, clean water, carbon storage, and dependable water supplies for towns and farms benefit nearby communities and the overall health of the planet. Non-wilderness areas of Olympic National Forest are managed under the Northwest Forest Plan to protect and restore old-growth forest habitat for spotted owls and marbled murrelets. Spotted owls live in old-growth forests; murrelets feed in coastal waters but nest in old-growth trees. The plan also takes measures to protect watersheds for salmon and other aquatic species as well as downstream uses. When adopted in 1994, it reduced the programmed timber harvest of Olympic National Forest by a third. After decades of unsustainable cutting, the forest is now managed primarily for restoration.

As a result of intensive logging, road building, and development outside these designated boundaries, the park and protected areas have become an ecological island. Wildlife migrations along river corridors, salmon and steelhead runs, and forest life cycles have become disrupted. Consequently, the celebrated biodiversity of the peninsula faces numerous threats. Nine Olympic wildlife species are federally listed as threatened under the Endangered Species Act. Along with spotted owls and marbled murrelets, five native fish stocks—Puget Sound chinook, Puget Sound steelhead, Hood Canal summer chum, Ozette Lake sockeye, and bull trout—are in critical condition. One candidate species and seven species of concern are also federally listed on the peninsula, and a single species, the

wolf, apex predator in Olympic forests, has been extirpated. Various recovery efforts are underway for listed salmon and steelhead stocks, and spotted owls and marbled murrelets are closely monitored. Spotted owls cope not only with historic loss of habitats but also displacement by non-native barred owls—to the point of little to no nesting success most years. Marbled murrelets, in spite of federal listing, continue to decline at a rate of more than 4 percent annually on the peninsula. These iconic creatures, irreplaceable in themselves, are indicators of the health of our old-growth forests and the viability of the Olympic ecosystem. Concern over their fate is deepened by the overriding threat posed by the climate crisis.

It's irrefutable that humans have altered the earth's atmosphere through heat-trapping gas emissions and

RIGHT **Northern spotted owl populations continue to decline in Olympic National Park and Olympic National Forest in spite of forest protections.** OPPOSITE **A marbled murrelet on a nest platform high in the forest canopy. These small seabirds fly up to fifty miles inland to nest in old-growth trees. With drastic population declines caused by the destruction of its nesting habitat, murrelets have been designated as a threatened species.**

Comparison photographs show the dramatic disappearance of Anderson Glacier due to global warming. TOP This 1936 photograph shows the glacier filling the basin south of Mount Anderson in Olympic National Park. BOTTOM Taken in 2015, this photograph depicts the melted-out basin with newly formed Moraine Lake occupying the landscape. Anderson Glacier is not unique. A 1982 survey documented 266 glaciers in the park. A follow-up survey in 2009 listed only 184 remaining; many were reduced in size. OPPOSITE Blue Glacier and Mount Olympus as photographed in 1979. Blue Glacier began a steady retreat in 1986 due to climate warming and has lost considerable mass since then.

Scientists have undertaken an ongoing research project to document the mass balance or annual gains and losses of Olympic glaciers. Ablation stakes are set along the length of glaciers each spring to measure annual accumulation and loss. Researchers also conduct monthly snow surveys in the Olympics during winter to predict water supply. TOP LEFT Using a portable steam drill, a park scientist installs ablation stakes in the upper Eel Glacier on Mount Anderson in Olympic National Park. The 40-foot-long stakes are placed at the point where the winter snowpack has reached its greatest depth. TOP RIGHT A park scientist threads his way between large crevasses on the upper reaches of Mount Olympus. Each fall, scientists scale the Blue Glacier to reach and measure ablation stakes that were inserted the previous spring. BOTTOM RIGHT Measuring an exposed length of an ablation stake on the lower Blue Glacier on Mount Olympus in early October. The amount of exposed stake indicates how much snow and ice melted on the glacier during summer months. BOTTOM LEFT Park scientists prepare for a winter snow survey at the Deer Park campground in Olympic National Park. Monthly snow measurements, used to forecast summer water supplies in the Dungeness River, have been taken at this site since 1948. The 75-year record provides a sobering picture of a changing winter snowpack, which has decreased by nearly 60 percent.

destructive land use practices. According to the Intergovernmental Panel on Climate Change, atmospheric greenhouse gasses are higher now than at any time in the past two million years. Human-caused warming increased the earth's temperature about one degree Celsius, two degrees Fahrenheit, over the past century. Analysis by the University of Washington Climate Impacts Group projects increases in average temperature for the Pacific Northwest from one to three degrees Celsius by the 2040s and one and a half to five and a half degrees Celsius by the 2080s. Climate change is bearing down on the Olympic Peninsula like a storm. Warming occurs in all seasons, with the largest increases in summer. Wetter winters and winter storms are more common, as are dryer summers. Warmer, droughty summers have led to increased wildfires, and more precipitation is falling as rain rather than snow. Reduced mountain snowpacks are contributing to lower flows and warmer waters in salmon streams in late summer and fall. Rain-on-snow events trigger more frequent and destructive floods. Increased carbon loading has led to ocean acidification, posing threats to shellfish, and warmer waters increase algal blooms, which can cause toxicity in shellfish. Rising seas accelerate erosion along coastal bluffs. With the obvious harm a warming climate poses to the Olympic ecosystem, the mainstays of the peninsula's economy—domestic and industrial water supplies, fisheries, agriculture, forestry, recreation, and tourism—are put at risk. Pointedly, tribes, coastal communities, and those most dependent on natural resources are experiencing the most immediate effects.

To get a sense of changes underway in the Olympics, I checked in with Bill Baccus. I first met Bill when he came to Olympic National Park in 1986 to do volunteer restoration work. Since then, as a park scientist, he has been involved in monitoring mountain lakes, coastal intertidal areas, air quality, glaciers, and annual mountain snowpacks. In winter, he skis in to four backcountry sites each month to measure snow depths and moisture content. This and his work monitoring mountain glaciers as part of a three-park research project led by Dr. Jon Riedel of North Cascades National Park have given him a frontline view of

how climate change is affecting the physical environment of the Olympics.

"The changes have been dramatic," Bill told me. The Olympics are relatively warm mountains, but they receive tremendous amounts of snow. The snowpack, he explained, is an important reservoir that feeds and cools streams in summer. Snow that doesn't melt year after year forms glaciers, so glaciers are great indicators of temperature and precipitation as well as climate trends. "The Olympic Mountains have lost a lot of ice," he said. In 2010 and 2017, Bill was part of a team of park service and university scientists that followed up on a 1982 glacier

**Trapped to extinction in the Olympics for their luxurious pelts, fishers were extirpated from the peninsula by the 1940s. But fishers are a success story. They were reintroduced to the park beginning in 2008 and have since established home territories throughout the peninsula's forests.**

inventory. Using annual data and aerial photography, they documented a 46 percent decrease in the area covered by glaciers in the Olympics and a loss of 118 glaciers, about a third of the Olympics' glaciers. "Ferry Glacier in the Bailey Range became Iceberg Lake, and Anderson, Lillian, and other once-familiar glaciers are virtually gone," Bill told me. He mentioned that south-facing glaciers have been hit particularly hard, losing 77 percent of their ice during this time; north-facing glaciers saw a 23 percent decrease in size. All Olympic glaciers took a hit; "compared with what we are seeing in the North Cascades or at Mount Rainier, it's happening much faster here."

Detailed annual surveys are now focused on two glaciers, the Blue Glacier on Mount Olympus and the Eel Glacier on Mount Anderson. Winter snowpack is measured in spring, stakes are set at different elevations on the glaciers, and crews return in fall to measure snow and ice melt. The data correlate to river flows and overall climate trends. Bill pointed me to data from 2015, a year of record warming that scientists consider a "stress-test" year for climate change. "The winter was on average four degrees Fahrenheit warmer than normal. Precipitation was close to normal, but it fell on all but the highest mountains as rain," he recalled. "When we did our snow surveys in April, a time of maximum snowpack, some of the areas we surveyed were bare." He said snowpack was normal above 6,500 feet, but glaciers below this elevation lost large amounts of ice that year. When he projects the 2015 data out into University of Washington climate models, it aligns with predictions for 2060. I recalled 2015 was the year the lightning-sparked Paradise Fire burned 2,800 acres of Queets rain forest. "We're in a precarious position in the Olympics," Bill emphasized, and it's undeniable. Unless we can slow the rate of warming, our glaciers, snowpacks, rivers, coastal areas, and the entire ecosystem will suffer. Indeed, a 2022 study predicts the demise of Olympic Mountain glaciers by 2070—fewer than fifty years.

Scientists and resource managers from the park and national forest identified alpine and subalpine meadows, wetlands, streams, and temperate rain forests as

to Olympic landscapes brings benefits as well. Wildfire rejuvenates forest ecosystems, creates new habitats, and results in mosaics across the landscape that hedge the extent of future fires. As one fire manager observed, the more fires that burn now, the better off we'll be in the future.

Wildlife also responds to warming in different ways. Animals that depend on specialized or sensitive habitats are more vulnerable than more generalist species. Amphibians that dwell in tributary streams, wetlands, and ponds such as endemic Olympic torrent and Van Dyke's salamanders and Cascades frogs are of particular concern as early melt and drought shrinks their habitats. Clark's nutcrackers will fare poorly as whitebark pines continue to die off due to blister rust, and threatened Taylor's checkerspot and Makah copper butterflies could lose open breeding habitats. An Audubon study warns of the potential loss of nineteen nesting bird species in Olympic National Park.

On the other hand, "generalists," animals that use a range of habitats during their life histories, will fare better. Black bear, Roosevelt elk, black-tailed deer, and snowshoe hare are more likely to adapt to climate-driven changes by adjusting ranges and seasonal movements. But this is true only if wildlife corridors can be maintained or established between diverse habitats and ownerships. A larger question is the long-term genetic exchange of animals to and from the peninsula's island-like habitat. When fishers were trapped out from Olympic old-growth forests in the 1920s, it took a multiagency and tribal effort to reintroduce the forest predators eighty years later. Key species such as martens, cougars, and bobcats may face genetic isolation as population density and development increase along the Interstate 5 corridor and southern peninsula. The likelihood of wolves migrating from the Cascades to the Olympics, for instance, is slim. And though Roosevelt elk thrive in a range of habitats, their long-term separation

ABOVE **The beautiful Taylor's checkerspot is an endangered butterfly found only in the Pacific Northwest. A few populations are protected on dry meadows and balds in Olympic National Forest.** OPPOSITE **This large male cougar was captured, radio collared, and released on the Hoko River as part of the Olympic Cougar Project. Cougars are skilled hunters and are the primary predators of elk and deer on the peninsula.**

particularly vulnerable to a warming climate. Dwindling snowpacks threaten the quality and extent of meadows as early snowmelt allows trees to encroach on subalpine habitats. Meadow-dwelling Olympic marmots are a particular concern. Marmot populations have declined in past decades, and climate change along with coyote predation were identified among the causes. Other endemic mammals, like the Olympic snow mole and Mazama pocket gopher, and numerous rare and endemic plants are also keyed to alpine habitats and could suffer in a warming world. Decreased mountain berry crops could impact some birds as well.

Lower down in the forests, warmer temperatures and summer drought affect different tree species in different ways. In general, warming and reduced soil moisture stress trees, making them vulnerable to attack by mountain pine beetles or balsam woolly adelgids and subject to a number of diseases. Summer drought and stressed trees lead to more severe wildfires, as has been evident in the Olympics in recent years. Beginning in 2003, fire intensity kicked up on the peninsula; fires occurred more frequently and burned larger areas. The return of more frequent fires

Taft Creek, a clear, spring-fed stream close to the Hoh Rain Forest Visitor Center and interpretive trails, is an excellent place to observe coho salmon in the fall.

from their evolutionary partner, the wolf, may portend problems. Elk in the park tend to be older than populations elsewhere, and a bacterial hoof disease that has affected herds in southwest Washington has begun to appear in Olympic elk. Natural control (predation of aged and weakened animals by wolves) is the obvious solution. Given the central role wolves play in maintaining health and viability of elk—and the uncertainties ahead—restoring wolves to the Olympics is of critical importance.

Perhaps most dramatically, climate change has altered the dynamics and flow regimes of Olympic rivers. Early snowmelt, melting glaciers, a historic rise in storm-driven floods, and increased sediment loads have degraded some rivers. These climate-driven conditions have widened river channels and aggravated channel braiding since the mid-1970s. Water temperatures and low flows also affect fish habitat. This all adds up to predicted declines in freshwater habitat for many peninsula fish populations. The current trend of ongoing habitat restoration is essential if we're to save one of the peninsula's most important resources.

Where streams flow into seas around the peninsula, climate is altering marine areas in fundamental ways. Atmospheric carbon dioxide dissolves in the ocean and causes seawater to become more acidic, about 30 percent more than pre-industrial times. Acidification hinders the ability of shelled animals such as mussels, clams, oysters, and crabs to form shells. Warmer water temperatures are associated with sea star wasting syndrome. That disease is fortunately in decline, but it may have eliminated iconic sunflower stars from the outer coast.

As climate change gathers like a storm over the peninsula, researchers and resource managers are scrambling to recover species and restore habitats. Nearly every scientist I spoke with is in agreement: a primary necessity is to maintain and restore the health and function of natural systems as the Olympic ecosystem enters an uncertain future. Fortunately, peninsula tribes, rural communities and municipalities, government agencies, land trusts, farmers, timber interests, environmental organizations, watershed groups, salmon coalitions, and a small army of citizen volunteers are stepping up to the challenge. ❖

TOP LEFT Garter snakes love to bask in the sun in open areas and skitter off into the leaves when disturbed. They feed on slugs, worms, and small amphibians.  TOP RIGHT Banana slugs prefer moist, shady forests, which are plentiful on the peninsula. They feed on numerous species of fungi and plants.  LEFT Damp forests of the peninsula's western valleys are a haven for amphibians. A northern red-legged frog blends with maple leaves and moss in Olympic National Park's Quinault Valley.  OPPOSITE LEFT Cascades frogs are found in the Cascades and Olympic Mountains, usually above 2,000 feet in elevation, where they favor ponds and small pools along streams.  OPPOSITE RIGHT Small, slender, western red-backed salamanders are widespread and common in woodlands and occur from sea level to over 3,000 feet in elevation. They favor seepages and streams and are often found beneath decaying wood or under rocks.

# Rain Forest Transcendence

If you plug in "Olympic Peninsula" on Google Maps and select satellite view, almost everything that isn't a mountaintop appears green. It's noted in Google Maps' accompanying text that the peninsula has "glaciers, rain forest & waterfalls in National Park known for Roosevelt elks [sic] & flying squirrels." Yes, the park has all of those things, but its rain forests are its truly distinguishing feature, rife with life and breathtakingly gorgeous.

Montane rain forests—sometimes called cloud forests—can be found in Costa Rica, New Zealand, Cambodia, Borneo, the Philippines, the Congo Basin, Sri Lanka, and elsewhere. Many are equatorial and tropical, which means they're very different from the Olympic rain forest, situated, as it is, at a temperate latitude. All are rooted in local political frameworks, specific histories, distinctive ecologies, and singular cultural contexts. As much as they incite in us certain common reactions, no two are the same in content or meaning.

When we hear "rain forest," a lot of us think of the Amazon. Like all rain forests, it's a territory of possible transcendence and a symbol of life itself. Hollywood has mined such rain forest resonances, partly via its *Twilight* franchise (five films that have jointly grossed billions), based on novels set on the Olympic Peninsula and suggesting to viewers that a rain forest is a likely place for vampires, werewolves, and romance. As popular as *Twilight* has been, though, it pales in comparison to *Avatar*, which is set in a dream-tinted version of a rain forest and is among the highest-grossing films of all time. *Avatar* is a tale of conflict in which the rain forest is imbued with moral force and spiritual depth, as it is for so many of us, even if we've never visited one, and even if we're not aware of its effect on us.

*Avatar* illuminates how rain forests work in human consciousness. In order to travel to the one in the film, its protagonist must undergo a ritualized transformation that casts him into an alternative reality and frees him from his corporeal self. His is a dream-like mythic journey story—a journey, at one level, into a subconscious realm. Eventually he comes to experience rain forest destruction as a personal wound he can't bear and must fight against. In his world, as in ours, it's not just the rain forest that's at stake when it's imperiled. Our spiritual lives and our inner worlds are imperiled, too.

—David Guterson

ABOVE **Bracken ferns are common in the Olympic rain forest. Large and fast-growing, they can dominate meadows in lowlands and mountain valleys.**
OPPOSITE **A small stream threads its way between moss-covered rocks in the Hoh Valley.**

ABOVE LEFT **Cauliflower mushroom (*Sparassis crispa*)** ABOVE
CENTER **Varnish shelf conk (*Ganoderma tsugae*)** ABOVE
RIGHT **Turkey tail fungus (*Trametes versicolor*)** RIGHT **Angel wings
(*Pleurotus porrigens*)** OPPOSITE TOP LEFT **Golden chanterelle
mushrooms (*Cantharellus cibarius*)** OPPOSITE TOP RIGHT **Fly amanita
(*Amanita muscaria*)** OPPOSITE BOTTOM RIGHT **Chicken of the woods
(*Laetiporus sulphureus*)** OPPOSITE BOTTOM LEFT **Crimson coral
fungus (*Ramaria araiospora var. rubella*)**

Dead and down trees in old-growth forests are an important part of ecosystem process. They retain moisture in dry times and provide habitat for small mammals, amphibians, and invertebrates. Decomposing logs host fungi and bacteria that break down organic compounds and make them available to other plants.

# Always Start with a Story

*Francine Swift et. al., Port Gamble S'Klallam Tribe*

## The Clallam Strong Men
### A Story of How the Clallams Got Their Name

Bruce is a little boy who lives with his family by the Elwha River near Port Angeles.
Others of his tribe live at Jamestown and Port Gamble.
They are called Clallam Indians, too.
The name means "Strong People."
This story tells how they got their name.

It happened a long time ago when Bruce's grandfather's grandfather was a little boy.
  Everything was very different then.
There were no towns and no stores, only Indians and Indian villages.
The Indians lived in longhouses, and their clothing was made from cedar bark.
One day, they had a big feast.
Many Indians came.
They ate salmon, clams, wild berries, and lots of good things from the woods.
Then they had a contest to see who was the strongest.
They decided to see who could lift a big log to the top of a house they were building.
"Who can lift this big log?" they asked.
All of the other Indian people tried to lift the big log.
Each tribe chose their strongest men.
None of them could lift the big log.
Then Bruce's people made a plan.
They remembered that logs float in water.
They rolled the big log into the water. When they reached the longhouse, everyone lifted
  at the same time and they put the log on top.
All of the other Indians thought that Bruce's people must be very strong to put the log
  up so high.
They all shouted "Clallam, Clallam," which means strong people. Ever since then, Bruce's
  people have been called Clallam Indians.

## Remembering a Few Words from Ted George
### Tribal History Development Ideas

*Ted George*
*November 5, 2008*

HISTORIES ARE WRITTEN BY WINNERS. INDIAN HISTORIES ARE AN OMISSION AND CRITICAL ELEMENT WE MUST WRITE.

WE MUST UNDERSTAND THE DYNAMICS AND DESTRUCTIVE FEATURES THAT BROUGHT ON OUR DARK AGE. A FULL RECOVERY DEMANDS THAT WE KNOW THAT STORY, ITS DAMAGES, ERRORS, AND WHAT WE MUST DO TO RESTORE THE VIABILITY OF OUR PEOPLE AND THIS PLACE.

WE ARE RESTORING OUR SELF-SUFFICIENCY, GOVERNANCE, AND TAKING CARE OF OUR OWN. COMINGLING OUR TRADITIONAL COMMUNITY CULTURES, VALUES, NATURAL SUPPORT SYSTEMS, TRIBALIZING, AND ECONOMIC HEALTH AND DIVERSITY REFLECT MANY OF THESE FEATURES.

THESE EMERGED FROM THOUSANDS OF YEARS OF COMMUNAL LIVING AND THE PRINCIPLES OF THESE MAY REPRESENT THE BEST COURSE FOR ALL PEOPLE. VINE DELORIA, JR., NOTED SIOUX AUTHOR, STATED THAT INDIAN PEOPLE CAN SHOW THE REST OF THE WORLD HOW TO LIVE.

US, STATE, AND LOCAL HISTORIES HAVE TOTALLY IGNORED OUR PASTS—OFTEN VIEWING OUR SURVIVAL LIFESTYLE AS OF OUR OWN CHOOSING—WITH MANY NEGATIVE CHARACTERIZATIONS.

WE KNOW THAT ABORIGINAL PEOPLE HERE LIVED IN SUCH PLENTY, THAT EASE OF MEETING NEED EXCEEDED MOST OTHERS. IT WAS AFTER "DISCOVERY" THAT OUR DECLINES, SURVIVAL MODES, AND IMPOSED "CIVILIZING" PRACTICES PUT AMERICAN INDIANS AT THE LOWEST LEVEL IN MOST NEGATIVE MEASURES.

HOPE IS THE FIRST PREREQUISITE FOR POSITIVE CHANGE. OUR TRUE HISTORIES MUST FEATURE THE POSITIVE ASPECTS: PRIDE, HONOR, AND THE UNIQUENESS OF EACH PERSON AND THEIR GIFTS—TALENTS, NAMINGS, POTLATCHES, RITES OF PASSAGE, HARMONY AND BALANCE, GENEROSITY, CARING FOR ALL, HEROES, MILESTONE EVENTS, AND MORE.

THE ORGANIZATION OF THIS MUST BE CREATED SO DATA, LOGIC, ORDER, AND SYSTEMIZING CONFORM TO THE PLANS.

THIS INCLUDES PURPOSE, PROCESS, FORMATS, LEADERSHIP, SUBJECT MATTERS, SOURCES, TAPING (VIDEO, ETC.) USAGES, . . .

## Looking Forward

Fishing life slept until the people awakened it with the Boldt Decision. Living on a reservation put marginal borders on our lives. The Boldt Decision opened borders to practice our treaty rights reserved by our ancestors. Today we travel the waters our ancestors traveled to harvest salmon, crab, shrimp, halibut, and geoduck to provide for our families. We work with Washington state to regulate our fisheries. Our tribe practices sovereignty—the God-given authority to govern our land and people. We are the host people of our land and territories.

Some of our fisheries have changed over the decades. Memories of fishing for bottom fish as plenty in the Hood Canal are but a memory. Gathering sea urchins on her shores are a memory. The Hood Canal Bridge stops orca from hunting salmon, their staple diet in the Hood Canal. They have recently reappeared in Port Gamble Bay.

We harvest manilas, oysters, and steamers in the Hood Canal region and the Strait of Juan de Fuca. Some of our people have a saying, "Hoko River to Hamma Hamma," which is a short description of a usual and accustomed territory.

Tribal journeys awakened more recently in 1989. Our canoe, the *Kloomachin*, came to life from a cedar log harvested from the US Forest Service. She was carved from a single cedar log for the Paddle to Seattle, organized by Emmett Oliver, Quinault, joined by our tribal chair, G. Jake Jones, with a delegation of S'Klallam tribal members and lead carver, Duane Pasco, non-Native, apprenticed by Canadian canoe carvers. We didn't know it, but the Paddle to Seattle awakened our ancestral highways, reviving networks of intertribal people in peace, feasting, friendships, song, dance, and strategic planning. Traveling the ancestral highways requires safety precautions among each canoe nation.

Our journeys have taken us as far as Bella Bella, British Columbia, for QATWAS (Heiltsuk, People Gathering Together) in 1993 and returning in 2014. *Kloomachin* made the first journey with a catamaran pilot boat. This crew witnessed feasting, singing, dancing, and history. They brought back a dream of our people building our own community longhouse.

Our longhouse birth was in 2004. The teachings that take place there are for our young people, elders, and families. We learn songs, dances, histories, language, protocols, and academic education in our longhouse. We learn to practice our best behavior and hospitality, and we listen to instruction from cultural leaders who practice S'Klallam language, songs, dances, and traditions. Other tribes visit on song and dance evenings to share a meal and enjoy intertribal songs and dances practiced publicly. We learn about the creators of the songs and the history of the songs

RIGHT **Princess Melody Bidtah offshore of the Port Gamble S'Klallam Reservation during the 1993 Paddle to Bella Bella** OPPOSITE **Ted George of the Port Gamble S'Klallam Tribe**

ABOVE LEFT **Bethany Swift and other Port Gamble S'Klallam tribal members push their canoe away from the shore at Point Julia as the canoe family gets underway during the Canoe Journey.** ABOVE RIGHT **Traditional clam feast cooked by Benji Ives** BOTTOM **Port Gamble S'Klallam queen Rea Ashworth looks toward the welcoming crowd as paddlers propel her tribal canoe to the beach at Tahola during the 2013 Paddle to Quinault canoe journey.** OPPOSITE LEFT **Crabber, Aletcia Ives** OPPOSITE TOP RIGHT **Mary Oliver and Andrew Ives in carving class** OPPOSITE BOTTOM RIGHT **Elder Ted Moran cleaning cedar bark in preparation for storage**

and dances we carry. Songs and names are property and guarded as such. Some are recent; some are traditional.

At home, our tribal government provide community services and businesses that allow for growth, development, and jobs—not only for S'Klallam but also for our local economy.

Art is important to the well-being of our people. A few focus on carving, painting, and design. Others create traditional cedar bark weavings. Yet others create wool weavings. These arts are honored as centerpieces on display throughout our tribal buildings. Others are worn as regalia in ceremony and celebration, made with love for family members and friends. Some are purchased, honoring the artist who makes the art. A noted artist is Jeffrey Veregge, who has art in the Smithsonian Institution's National Museum of the American Indian, the Burke Museum, Marvel comics, Disney feature films, and a long list of public credentials to his name.

Our tribe spends revenue on educating our young people. Our young people attend public schools. Some students engage readily with support of our tribal members in the school system. They see familiar faces who support them in their studies. Our preschool numbers increase, and their high school graduation rates are reflected. We do not live in isolation from the greater Kitsap community.

This engagement is also reflected in Little League sports and school sports. You will see our youth in basketball, baseball, wrestling, softball, football, volleyball, and track. You will see our youth mentioned in newspapers as strong athletic competitors. Our families strongly support their athletes in every area of competition they pursue. Our young ladies excel in basketball, volleyball, and softball; one became a wrestling champion of the state. Our young men excel in football, baseball, and track. Families follow their athletes to district, regional, state, and national competitions. Our community includes the North Kitsap/Kingston area.

Climate change, fentanyl, COVID-19, and pollution take the forefront of challenges faced by the S'Klallam people as well as the world. Our tribal leaders deal with these challenges as well as the rest of humanity.

LEFT **Wool weaving student Stormy Purser** RIGHT **Gina Steiner prepares gifts for potlatching at Seattle's Burke Museum for a celebration of art installations by two S'Klallam artists.**

Our fisheries focus on maintaining and preserving salmon runs, creeks, eelgrass, and habitat. Hatcheries perpetuate stock for future years. Clam beds are planted with seed from current FLUPSY technology. Heat waves impacted our beaches. The beaches were closed and remained closed for a considerable time after the intense heat killed our clams.

Health care providers strategized with tribal leaders to provide safety measures for our communities against COVID-19. Lockdown, quarantine, infection testing, immunization, handwashing, and masking became part of our routine practices and safeguards for the community at large. Communication became vitally important through 2020 and 2021. Our businesses had to implement health and safety practices to prevent the spread of COVID-19, as did our educational systems and service systems.

Public invitations go out in the way of advertisement. We welcome visitors to our casino, hotel, gas stations, convenience stores, and cannabis enterprises. We serve our public in our restaurants. Our seasonal business includes fireworks. Our tribal business is expanding to include private seafood buyers, licensing tribal members to sell seafood under tribal licensing.

Our current tribal endeavors show our tribal priorities:

- Elder housing
- A fishing boat launch
- Fisheries facilities and offices
- Wellness recovery houses
- A cannabis enterprise store
- Family lot development and housing

Our less visible investments include land buyback investments, such as the following:

- Port Gamble Forterra properties
- Hansville Block properties
- Washington State Department of Natural Resources
- Heronswood Gardens
- Kountry Korner properties, now The Point properties
- Other private properties

We look forward to developing acquisitions with an even eye on the future generations. We negotiate with private land investors, the US Navy, Washington state, and other entities. We remember the teachings of our elders, carry on traditional practices using medicines we learned growing up, and learn what we can of our Klallam language, our new and old songs, and our dances. We support our youth, trying to maintain a balance of new technology, lifeways, and traditional ways. Our fishermen live on the waters, our hunters gather from the mountains, and our clam diggers gather from healthy waterways. Our canoes travel our ancestral highways. We have something to share with our young people, and we hope our witnesses are pleased with our decisions.

## Land of the Noonday Sun, Noo-Kayet: How We Got This Name

The S'Klallam people held feasts. We hold formal feasts called potlatches. We are taught that to have a potlatch, there are four traditional rules:

1. We must have witnesses.
2. We must invite guests.
3. We must feed all guests.
4. We must gift each guest.

Gifts do not have to be extravagant, and it is important to personally invite your guests. We were told that in doing an invitation, it is a best practice to sing a song.

Our S'Klallam people were known for hospitality, food, and war. Our village was known for potlatching such bright fires in the night that the fires shone as bright as the noonday sun. The firepit still exists on the beach; even though the tide goes in and out decades later, still evidence of the fires of previous hosts remains. Others say that when the mill was opened, the lights shone bright as the noonday sun.

This material and periodical are by the Center for the Study of Migrant and Indian Education, a project of Central Washington State College. The project was funded by Health, Education and Welfare, US Office of Education, under Public Law 89-10, Title IV. Potlatch protocol was taught by Lester Greene, Makah; David Boxley, Tsimpsian; and Gene Jones, Sr., S'Klallam.

# The Way Ahead: Re-Storying the Landscape

## TIM MCNULTY

Tom Jay was a sculptor, poet, and essayist on the Olympic Peninsula. He was a devotee of rivers and streams and a passionate defender of wild salmon. Tom was also a friend, and I had the good luck to work with him on several conservation efforts over the years. We documented wildlife use on the Duckabush River and fought hydroelectric dams on the Duckabush and Dosewallips. When the last chum salmon were at risk in his home watershed of Chimacum Creek, Tom dove into restoration work. With his wife, Sara Johani, he founded Wild Olympic Salmon to celebrate wild fish and revive stream habitat; the group was the predecessor to today's North Olympic Salmon Coalition. In *Reaching Home: Pacific Salmon, Pacific People*, Tom wrote that restoration becomes "re-storying" the landscape, telling a new story of humans' relationship with the places where we live.

The past few decades have seen a blossoming of new stories across the peninsula landscape. Some are large watershed-scale restorations, while others are smaller community-based endeavors. All are working to restitch the ecological fabric of the peninsula, repair and reconnect habitats, and help creatures and natural processes become more resilient in the face of climate change. And all tell a renewed story of people, tribes, and communities working in consort with the natural world.

The beginnings of a natural logjam form along the North Fork Skokomish River in Olympic National Park. Logjams create ideal habitat for salmon.

## SKOKOMISH SUCCESS

THE SKOKOMISH RIVER DRAINS THE RUGGED SOUTHEAST CORNER OF THE OLYMpics and flows into Hood Canal. For decades, it was the first river in Washington to flood after heavy rains and the last to subside. A 1946 agreement between Olympic National

ABOVE **Rocks and falling water on the North Fork Skokomish River. Angular boulders in the riverbed create falls, pools, and riffles, hallmarks of a wild Olympic river.** OPPOSITE **A mature forest is filled with snags, down logs, and ferns along the North Fork Skokomish River in Olympic National Park.**

Forest and a private timber company granted exclusive logging rights to more than one hundred thousand acres of old-growth forest. When the agreement was terminated a half century later, the company had cut more than 3.5 billion board feet from the forest and left behind more than one thousand miles of logging roads carved into steep, unstable slopes. Fueled by more than ten feet of rain each year, road failures, landslides, and debris flows became common. Tributaries and river channels were choked with two million cubic yards of gravel. Salmon habitat was obliterated, and valley farmlands were regularly inundated by floodwaters. The Skokomish Indian Tribe, whose reservation is on the lower river, suffered the brunt of the destruction.

In the 1990s, the Northwest Forest Plan reset the management direction for Olympic National Forest, and the Skokomish was identified as a priority watershed. The US Forest Service began the herculean task of watershed restoration. One hundred miles of failing roads were removed, and slopes were stabilized. The agency was then joined by a powerful coalition that included the Skokomish Indian Tribe, state and local agencies, timber industry representatives, environmental organizations, the local conservation district, Grange, and others. They formed the Skokomish Watershed Action Team. All were committed to the goals of addressing failing roads in the upper watershed, reducing flooding, and restoring habitat for listed Chinook salmon and steelhead in the river. They secured funds through the US Forest Service's Legacy Roads and Trails program and other sources, and over the next decade they completed large-scale decommissioning, stabilization, and trail conversion of nearly two hundred miles of failing roads.

Mike Anderson represented the Wilderness Society in the effort. "After a decade of work, the Skokomish watershed went from an 'at risk' classification to 'properly functioning,'" Mike told me. "Flooding is greatly reduced, and destructive landslides have been stopped. But what's remarkable is that the Skokomish, once considered the poster child for damaged watersheds, is now a startling example of successful collaborative restoration." Salmon

are returning to both the north and south forks of the Skokomish, including sockeye to Lake Cushman for the first time in eighty years. Restoration continues in the lower river and estuary with a US Army Corps of Engineers project underway to move dikes away from the river to create wetlands and salmon rearing habitat and help accommodate floodwaters.

"The Skokomish was an early canary in the coal mine for climate-driven impacts on damaged watersheds," Mike reflected. "Collaborative efforts with a watershed focus like this one are a proven way to move forward."

## EXTENDING PROTECTION FOR THE HOH RIVER

**ACROSS THE MOUNTAINS, ANOTHER CONSERVATION** effort is restoring a thirty-mile river corridor between Olympic National Park and the Pacific coast. Beginning in 2004, the nonprofit Hoh River Trust worked with public and private partners to acquire more than six thousand acres of previously logged lands along the Hoh River, one of North America's greatest fisheries streams and home to some of the healthiest wild salmon runs outside Alaska. Concentrating on tributaries and side channels, the trust removed hundreds of fish-blocking culverts and erased over twenty miles of eroding log roads. Crews thinned streamside forests to restore diverse riparian habitats and encourage large conifers that would contribute to river-bank structure and fish habitat. Blocked and damaged side channels were restored for juvenile coho and steelhead that rear there year-round. Timberlands that were planted in even-aged, single-species crops were commercially thinned where needed to encourage diverse, late-successional habitats for wildlife and provide income to the trust. In time a network of old-growth habitats will extend the length of the Hoh River from the park to the coast.

In 2017, the Nature Conservancy took over the trust and expanded the restoration effort, bringing the total conservation lands on the Hoh to more than ten thousand acres. The conservancy continues to partner with tribes, local communities, and state agencies with shared goals to restore salmon to a harvestable abundance and improve recreational access while fostering a strong local economy. The Hoh River Recreation and Conservation Area aims to create a community forest that will allow economies and ecosystems to thrive together. The conservancy is also working to reconnect and retore habitat corridors in the Quillayute, Queets, and Quinault watersheds.

## ELWHA INSPIRATION

**ALONG THE MORE POPULATED NORTHERN SLOPE OF** the peninsula, the Elwha River dam removal claims the mantle of the largest salmon restoration project in the nation. As the river returns to its wild and free-flowing state, the ecological recovery is profound. The Elwha's legendary Chinook salmon are leading the way with increasing numbers returning yearly to the upper watershed. Steelhead are not far behind, and coho salmon are reclaiming a wide network of tributary streams. Logs freed from reservoirs are stacking up into logjams, creating pools and riffles for salmon and structuring channels. More than twenty million tons of sediments trapped behind the dams have replenished spawning areas and rebuilt the delta at the river mouth, revitalizing the nearshore environment. The Elwha has become a beacon of hope for damaged ecosystems everywhere.

Rather than overshadowing smaller restoration efforts, the Elwha's epic recovery has inspired them. As population grows along the Strait of Juan de Fuca, communities are increasingly learning to cherish, defend, and restore the natural places around them. Dozens of restoration projects have recovered salmon and wildlife habitat and improved water quality. As with the Elwha restoration, peninsula tribes have provided the vision and leadership for many of them. Tribes, resource agencies, local governments, salmon recovery groups, land trusts, conservation districts, farmers, fishers, landowners—and a sizable host

A young volunteer examines juvenile chum salmon fry in a plexiglass aquarium during a survey following the Jimmycomelately Creek ecosystem restoration on Sequim Bay.

of volunteers—have invested countless hours and tens of millions of dollars in public and private funds to bring peninsula watersheds back to health. Shorelines, estuaries, rivers, creeks, wetlands, forests, farmlands, clean water, and open space all benefit. Community-based watershed plans have cleaned up non-source pollution, resulting in healthier streams and the reopening of commercial shellfish beds. Once-industrialized estuaries and salt marsh habitats are being restored. Dikes are being moved, roads relocated, culverts replaced with bridges. Across the peninsula, critical habitats and recreation areas have been restored.

Near Quilcene, the Northwest Watershed Institute is working with the Jefferson Land Trust, property owners, and more than forty organizations to protect and restore the Tarboo Creek watershed from its headwaters to Dabob Bay. Within the Tarboo Wildlife Preserve, the institute has reconfigured streams and restored and replanted more than three hundred acres of wetland, floodplain, and forest. Once cleared and drained for agriculture, the preserve now provides habitat for a diversity of fish and wildlife as well as opportunities for ongoing programs in research and education. At the head of Sequim Bay, the Jamestown S'Klallam Tribe and more than two dozen partner organizations and agencies undertook an ambitious restoration of Jimmycomelately Creek and Estuary. Putting skills and equipment to work in a new economy, area contractors returned the creek to its historic meandering channel and reconnected it to its estuary, a former mill and log yard. The Highway 101 bridge was replaced and a road in the estuary was removed, along with culverts and pilings. More than fifty acres of salt marsh were restored. Restoration ecologist Dave Shreffler, who worked on the project, told me that in the two decades since the restoration began, federally listed summer chum salmon returns in the creek increased from seven to an average of more than two thousand annually.

West of Sequim Bay, the North Olympic Salmon Coalition undertook a massive restoration at the mouth of the Dungeness River. Typical of many estuaries on the peninsula, the area where Meadowbrook Creek enters the estuary had been diked, drained, filled, roaded, armored, and commercially developed. The Washington Department of Fish and Wildlife acquired the area, and work began to restore more than forty acres of coastal wetlands and a half mile of stream. The armored road was removed; another was redirected out of the estuary. A new bridge was constructed that can accommodate floods and highest tides. Derelict buildings were demolished and hauled

away, along with three hundred tons of contaminated soil and some five hundred tons of creosote-treated timbers, including the remains of a half-mile-long dock. Meadowbrook Creek was restored to its historic channel, new lagoons were created, and a wildlife viewing area was established that is immensely popular with birders.

Among the many partners at Meadowbrook Creek, the North Olympic Land Trust also conserves key forest, farm, and recreational lands on the north peninsula. Included in its protected properties is the beautiful Lyre River conservation area, which includes an estuary, streams, tide flats, and upland forest. The land trust's Elk Creek conservation area close to the town of Forks protects two miles of productive salmon stream and 250 acres of lowland and riparian forest.

## ACCESS, EDUCATION, RECOVERY

**NEARLY ALL THESE PROJECTS INCLUDE OPPORTUNI-**ties for public access and education. As the peninsula shifts from a traditional resource-based economy, recreation has become one of its fastest growing sectors, with tourism now accounting for nearly 20 percent of the area's economy. Traditional activities like fishing, hunting, hiking, and camping have always been central to the peninsula. The demise of the Milwaukee Railroad in the 1980s presented a new opportunity. In 1988 the Peninsula Trails Coalition was launched with the visionary goal of working across multiple jurisdictions and ownerships to establish a public access trail along the former railroad corridor from Port Townsend to the Pacific Ocean. Now entering its

fourth decade, the Olympic Discovery Trail is a remarkable success. The scenic, non-motorized trail traverses forests, rivers, pastures, and shorelines while passing through local, state, and national parklands as well as several restoration sites. About 70 percent of the 130-mile trail route is completed. A year-round boon to recreation, it attracts walkers, runners, bicyclists, and equestrians from around the region.

The re-storying of the peninsula has been greatly enhanced by natural resource agency outreach and educational programs offered by tribes, land trusts, conservation organizations, schools, and social clubs. Several place-based environmental education institutes are doing outstanding work with schools, youth programs, and adult offerings. NatureBridge on Lake Crescent, the Dungeness River Nature Center in Sequim, the Feiro Marine Life Center in Port Angeles, and the Port Townsend Marine Science

RIGHT **Young volunteers [Waverly Shreffler, Mathew and Jessica Craig, and Elliot and Hudson Soelter] haul debris from Kalaloch Beach in Olympic National Park during an annual volunteer Washington Coastal Cleanup sponsored by Washington CoastSavers.** OPPOSITE LEFT **A cougar is weighed as part of work-up by members of the collaborative research team include biologists Dave Manson (left), Andy Stratton of Panthera (middle), and Mike Sheldon of the Lower Elwha Klallam Tribe (right). This pioneering program works across state and tribal jurisdictional boundaries to conserve cougars on the Olympic Peninsula.** OPPOSITE RIGHT **Cougars captured and studied as part of the Olympic Cougar Project are sedated, blindfolded, monitored for respiration and temperature, weighed, measured and aged. Their DNA is sampled, and radio collars are fitted before they are released. Here Dave Manson, wildlife biologist with Lower Elwha Klallam Tribe, checks the fit of a radio collar.**

Where Meadowbrook Creek flows through the Dungeness River estuary, the land had been diked, drained, filled, roaded, armored, and commercially developed. The North Olympic Salmon Coalition spearheaded a massive restoration project, removing dikes and a road, and redirecting a second road out of the estuary. Buildings, contaminated soil, and creosoted pilings were removed to restore the creek to its historic channel, with restored wetlands and new lagoons. TOP LEFT Meadowbrook Creek restored to its original channel; TOP RIGHT The delta and estuary now function as prime fish and wildlife habitat. BOTTOM Floodwaters disperse across the delta. OPPOSITE Pebble Beach—sŋaʔŋáʔant cáwŋən ʔəssaqɬúŋt—in downtown Port Angeles offers beaches, walking paths, and a viewing platform.

Center, among others, are fostering a deeper appreciation of the beauty and biological complexity of terrestrial and marine ecosystems. Their work and the work of all the organizations mentioned above is shaping a vision for the future of this place in which the entire life community can flourish.

I count myself lucky that my time on the peninsula has coincided with this gradual shift toward ecological recovery. From my first glimpse of a sea otter, restored to the coast in 1970, to witnessing the reintroduction of the first fishers to the snowy Elwha Valley thirty-five years later, I've witnessed vital pieces of the Olympic puzzle fit back into place. Both species were hunted to extinction here a century ago, but not all wounds inflicted on the ecosystem were eliminations. In the 1920s, non-native mountain goats were introduced to the Olympic Mountains. They proliferated, disrupting meadow communities and impacting rare and endemic plants and native wildlife habitat. The National Park Service and cooperating agencies recently completed a multiyear project to remove goats from the park and national forest. Each species restoration and each removal of an invasive species strengthens the resilience of the Olympic ecosystem and shores up hope for the future. So much has been saved and recovered on the peninsula; it gives all of us hope that the work that remains can be accomplished.

The continued recovery of threatened and at-risk species is essential to restore robustness to ecosystems. The return of wolves, a keystone species and the only mammal missing from the Olympic ecosystem, should be a high priority. Important habitat lands, particularly low-elevation winter elk habitats, should be added to the park on a willing-seller basis as recommended by the park's general management plan and advocated by conservation organizations. Habitat protections and restoration of national forest lands, as guided by the Northwest Forest Plan, should be funded, monitored, and adjusted as conditions require. And Washington state forest lands, some 140,000 acres on the peninsula, should be managed with greater attention given to fish and wildlife habitat and, critically, to carbon storage.

THIS PAGE **Beginning in 2018, federal and state agencies, area tribes, and volunteers cooperated on a major mountain goat removal project. Goats were sedated and captured by helicopter crews, medically worked up, and transported by truck to the Cascades where native populations had failed to recover from overhunting.** OPPOSITE **Non-native mountain goats were brought to the Olympics by hunting interests in the 1920s. Foraging, trampling, and creating wallows in richly vegetated alpine areas was recognized as a problem as the goat population grew. Studies to document impacts and find a solution began in the 1970s.**

An extraordinary opportunity for carbon storage exists on the peninsula's state- and privately owned forest lands. Numerous studies indicate that mature and "legacy" forests—older stands that originated naturally following disturbances or logging—sequester vast amounts of carbon above and below ground. Washington Forest Defense, Pacific Northwest Climate Alliance, and other groups are working to preserve older forests on Washington Department of Natural Resources land and promote economic opportunity in rural communities. An enlightened program of tax incentives and compensation would also encourage private forest owners to manage for longer cutting rotations and larger trees. These measures would benefit fish and wildlife habitat, clean water and air, recreation opportunities, and promote community stability. Importantly, they would aid in the fight against global warming.

Ultimately, to thrive during climate change, improved habitat connectivity between the Olympics and the Cascades wildlife areas needs to be reestablished. The Interstate 5 corridor and growth in the Chehalis Valley hinder the exchange of animals and genetic diversity between the two regions. Conservation Northwest's Cascades to Olympics program is working to reestablish connectivity by restoring habitats and improving wildlife crossings along the Interstate 5 corridor and US Highway 12 in the Chehalis River Basin. Because 85 percent of Washington's wildlife species utilize riparian areas, the preliminary focus is on river corridors.

The deeper importance of the Olympic Peninsula extends beyond the beauty and biological richness of this island-like ecosystem. It lies in the promise these lands and waters offer to the Northwest region, the North Pacific Rim, and the world. The peninsula was once a place where human society got it right. It could be again. Imagine a place where humans can rediscover old and new ways to live sustainably with the larger community of life—and share those relationships with a world hungry for a new story. ❖

Autumn reflections in the Wynoochee River

# Olympic Climate Action Tips

Olympic Climate Action seeks a safe, prosperous, sustainable future for residents of the Olympic Peninsula by addressing the threat of climate change. We all have a critical part to play in this important effort.

1. Recognize that we all directly or indirectly emit far too much toxic and greenhouse gas emissions due to our society's fossil-fuel dependence.
2. Calculate your carbon footprint to see where you stand in relation to a sustainable human society and then create a plan to halve your household footprint while saving money, within ten years (or less): Berkeley's "Cool Climate" Calculator (coolclimate.org/calculator) takes about an hour. Carbon Footprint Ltd. (carbonfootprint.com) allows you to buy offsets after you calculate your footprint.
3. In the kitchen: Eat local; eat mostly plants; avoid food waste.
4. On the road: Drive less (walk, bike, bus, carpool). Buy or lease a zero-emission vehicle (ZEV) to replace one ICE (internal combustion engine) car.
5. In the air: Cut your air travel in half.
6. At home: Upgrade your house envelope (better insulation, doors, windows; roughly 3–10 percent); add smart devices to reduce energy consumption; install an electric heat pump and a heat-pump water heater; install solar panels or buy green electricity. See energy.gov for more details.
7. In the community: Organize a community solarization project (powertripenergy .com). Volunteer to help calculate the carbon footprint for others; support renewable energy programs with all local agencies.
8. Use your voice! Share your concerns with friends, neighbors, and acquaintances in conversations. Be informed and contact your elected officials and community leaders with your expectations and hold them accountable.
9. Use your resources. Invest in community endeavors, leaders, businesses, and investment funds that are working to address climate change.
10. Join Olympic Climate Action (olyclimate.org/actions/), Local 20/20 (L2020.org), or other local activist groups working with others to reduce not only your own, but also our society's carbon footprint!

**Bull kelp washes ashore at Point of the Arches in Olympic National Park.**

A visitor pauses to admire epiphyte-draped bigleaf maples on the Hall of Mosses Trail in Olympic National Park's Hoh Rain Forest. Over 130 species of canopy epiphytes—mosses, lichens, liverworts, and ferns—have been identified in the Hoh Valley.

# Acknowledgments

This book would not have been possible without the support, insights, and introductions provided by Steve Robinson. Other key advocates for the project included Larry Workman, Tom Uniack, Mark Glyde, Rob Smith, Donna Osseward, and Governor Dan Evans, as well as David Guterson and Lynda V. Mapes.

Wendy Sampson (Lower Elwha Klallam Tribe) was the first tribal member to join our team, and she remained a steadfast supporter—and contributor—throughout the long process of making a book. In addition to all the tribal contributing writers featured in these pages, other tribe members offered encouragement and support including Larry Ralston, Justine James Jr., Lia Frenchman, Naomi Brandenfels, and Aiyana Underwood (Quinault Tribe); Janine Ledford and Tim Greene (Makah Tribe); Marie Hebert (Port Gamble S'Klallam Tribe); Ron Allen and Ann Sargent (Jamestown S'Klallam Tribe); and the Olympic Peninsula Intertribal Cultural Advisory Committee (OPICAC). *Native Peoples of the Olympic Peninsula: Who We Are, Second Edition*, edited by Jacilee Wray, was a helpful resource.

The following individuals—representing several federal, state, and local agencies, tribes, colleges and universities, conservation organizations, and community members—all generously shared their time and expertise with writer Tim McNulty, and provided him invaluable assistance during the researching and writing of his essays: Mike Anderson, Bill Baccus, Ed Bowlby, Sam Brenkman, Janis Burger, Ed Chadd, David Conca, Steve Fradkin, Connie Gallant, Patti Happe, Mike Hagen, Roger Hoffman, Gay Hunter, Kurt Jenkins, Mike McHenry, Bruce Moorhead, Jose Paul, Jim Pearson, Kate Reavey, Tom Sanford, Janet Scharf, Autumn Scott, Dave Shreffler, Darrell Smith, and Brian Stewart.

# Appreciation

**Braided River** gratefully acknowledges the financial support and friendship of the following organizations that helped to make this publication and media campaign possible.

**Olympic Park Advocates** is a grass-roots citizens conservation organization dedicated to protecting and restoring the wilderness and ecological integrity of Olympic National Park and the Olympic ecosystem.

For 75 years, OPA has worked diligently to defend this magnificent planetary preserve and its surrounding wildlands through research, education, and advocacy. Today we are redoubling our efforts in the face of climate change and increasing human demands. We invite you to join us. Visit our website at olympicparkadvocates.org. OPA is a 501(c)3 not-for-profit organization.

**The National Parks Conservation Association** is the voice of America's national parks, working for more than a century to protect and preserve our nation's most iconic and inspirational places. Thanks to this advocacy and the work of many others, the unique ecosystem within Olympic National Park remains resilient and protected, for the enjoyment of ours and future generations. Find out more at www.npca.org.

# Further Reading and Notes

## Further Reading

Aldwell, Thomas T. *Conquering the Last Frontier*. Seattle: Artcraft Engraving and Electrotype Co., 1950.

Beres, Nancy, Mitzi Chandler, and Russ Dalton, eds. *Island of Rivers: An Anthology Celebrating 50 Years of Olympic National Park*. Seattle: Pacific Northwest National Parks and Forests Association, 1988.

Dietrich, William. *The Final Forest: The Battle for the Last Great Trees of the Pacific Northwest*. New York: Simon & Schuster, 1992.

Gorsline, Jerry, ed. *Shadows of Our Ancestors: Readings in the History of Klallam-White Relations*. Port Townsend, WA: Empty Bowl,1992.

Kirk, Ruth. *Ozette: Excavating a Makah Whaling Village*. Seattle: University of Washington Press, 2015.

Kirk, Ruth and Jerry Franklin. *The Olympic Rain Forest: An Ecological Web*. Seattle: University of Washington Press, 1992.

Lien, Carsten, ed. *Exploring The Olympic Mountains: Accounts of the Earliest Expeditions 1878–1890*. Seattle: Mountaineers Books, 2001.

Lien, Carsten. *Olympic Battleground: The Power Politics of Timber Preservation*. San Francisco: Sierra Club Books, 1991.

——. *Olympic Battleground: Creating and Defending Olympic National Park*, 2nd edition. Seattle: Mountaineers Books, 2000. Mapes, Lynda V. *Breaking Ground: The Lower Elwha Klallam Tribe and the Unearthing of Tse-whit-zen Village*. Seattle: University of Washington Press, 2009.

——. *Elwha: A River Reborn*. Seattle: Mountaineers Books, 2013.

Matthews, Daniel. *Natural History of the Pacific Northwest Mountains*. Portland, OR: Timber Press, 2017.

McNulty, Tim. *Olympic National Park: A Natural History*, 4th edition. Seattle: University of Washington Press, 2018.

Morgan, Murray. *The Last Wilderness: A History of the Olympic Peninsula*. Seattle: University of Washington Press, 2019.

Olympic Mountain Rescue. *Olympic Mountains: A Climbing Guide*. Seattle: Mountaineers Books, 2006.

Olympic Peninsula Intertribal Cultural Advisory Committee (OPICAC), edited by Jacilee Wray. *Native Peoples of the Olympic Peninsula: Who We Are*, 2nd edition. Norman, OK: University of Oklahoma Press, 2015.

Parratt, Smitty. *Gods and Goblins: A Field Guide to Place Names of Olympic National Park,* 2nd edition. Forks, WA: Poseidon Peak Publishing, 2009.

Peterson, Gary, and Glynda Schaad. *Women to Reckon With: Untamed Women of the Olympic Wilderness*. Forks, WA: Poseidon Peak Publishing, 2007.

Reid, Joshua L. *The Sea Is My Country: The Maritime World of the Makahs*. New Haven, NJ: Yale University Press, 2018.

Romano, Craig. *Day Hiking Olympic Peninsula*, 2nd edition. Seattle: Mountaineers Books, 2016.

Rooney, Jack R. *Frontier Legacy: History of the Olympic National Forest 1897-1960*. Seattle: Northwest Interpretive Association, 1997.

Smith, LeRoy. *Pioneers of the Olympic Peninsula*. Port Angeles, WA: Olympic Graphic Arts, Inc., 1976.

Steelquist, Robert. *The Northwest Coastal Explorer: Your Guide to the Places, Plants, and Animals of the Pacific Coast*. Portland, OR: Timber Press, 2016.

Sullivan, Robert. *A Whale Hunt: Two Years on the Olympic Peninsula with the Makah and Their Canoe*. New York: Scribner, 2000.

Swan, James. *The Northwest Coast*. New York: Harper and Brothers, 1857 Seattle: University of Washington Press, 1992.

Wood, Robert L. *Across the Olympic Mountains: The Press Expedition, 1889-90*. Seattle: Mountaineers Books, 1989.

——. *The Land That Slept Late: The Olympic Mountains in Legend and History*. Seattle: Mountaineers Books, 1995.

——. *Olympic Mountains Trail Guide*. Seattle: Mountaineers Books, 1984.

Wood, Robert, and Bill Hoke. *Olympic Mountains Trail Guide*, 4th edition. Seattle: Mountaineers Books, 2020.

## Notes

### Mountains of the Sea

Gavin, Daniel G, David M. Fisher, Erin M. Herring, Ariana White, and Linda B. Brubaker, "Paleoenvironmental Change on the Olympic Peninsula, Washington: Forests and Climate from the Last Glaciation to the Present," Final Report to Olympic National Park (2003).

Halofsky, Jessica E., D. Peterson, K. O'Halloran, and C. Hawkins Hoffman, eds., "Adapting to Climate Change at Olympic National Forest and Olympic National Park." Gen. Tech. Rep. PNW-GTR-844. (Portland, OR.: US Department of Agriculture, Forest Service, Pacific Northwest Research Station, 2011).

Jenkins, Kurt, Andrea Woodward, and Ed Schreiner, "A Framework for Long-term Ecological Monitoring in Olympic National Park: Prototype for the Coniferous Forest Biome." Information and Technology Report. (Reston, VA: US Department of the Interior and US Geological Survey, 2003).

McCaffery, R., and K. Jenkin, eds., "Natural Resource Condition Assessment: Olympic National Park." Natural Resource Report NPS/OLYM/NRR—2018/1826, (Fort Collins, CO: National Park Service, 2018).

Miller, Ian M., Caitlin Shishido, Liam Antrim, and C. Edward Bowlby, "Climate Change and the Olympic Coast National Marine Sanctuary: Interpreting Potential Futures." (Washington DC: US Department of Commerce National Oceanic and Atmospheric Administration, Office of National Marine Sanctuaries, 2013).

Roop, H.A., G.S. Mauger, H. Morgan, A.K. Snover, and M. Krosby, "Shifting Snowlines and Shorelines: The Intergovernmental Panel on Climate Change's Special Report on the Ocean and Cryosphere and Implications for Washington State," (Briefing paper prepared by the Climate Impacts Group, University of Washington, Seattle, WA, 2020): doi.org/10.6069/KTVN-WY66.

Rothman, Hal K., "American Eden: The Administrative History of Olympic National Park," Unpublished Report, (US Department of Interior, National Park Service, 2005).

US Department of Interior, National Park Service. "Olympic National Park, Washington, Final Mountain Goat Management Plan/Environmental Impact Statement," (Port Angeles, WA: National Park Service, 2018).

### Qʷidičča?a·tx̌ (Qwih-dich-chuh-ahtX), or "People of the Cape"

Makah Tribal Council. 1995. *Makah Cultural & Research Center Museum Exhibit Leaflet.* Second Edition. Neah Bay, WA: Makah Tribal Council.

Pascua, Maria. 2022. *Makah Language Dialogues.* Port Angeles, WA: Makah Cultural & Research Center Museum with Penprint.

Samuels, Stephan. 1994. *Ozette Archaeology Project Research Reports, Volume II: Fauna.* Contributors, David R. Huelsbeck, Gary C. Wessen, and Raymond T. DePuydt. Washington State University Department of Archaeological Research Reports of Investigation 66. Seattle, WA: National Park Service, Northwest Regional Office.

Stewart, Hilary. 1987. *The Adventures and Sufferings of John R. Jewitt, Captive of Maquinna, Annotated and Illustrated by Hilary Stewart.* Vancouver, BC/Toronto, ON: Douglas and McIntyre.

### Klallam Language Revitalization

CivicPlus Content Management System. n.d. "Facilities: Pebble Beach Park." City of Port Angeles, Washington. Accessed April 3, 2023. www.cityofpa.us/Facilities/Facility/Details/West-End-Park-44.

Gupta, Sanjay. 1996. "Balancing and Checking." In *Essays on Modern Democracy,* edited by Bob Towsky, 36–48. Brook Stone Publishers.

Lower Elwha Klallam Tribe. 2018. "Point No Point Treaty, 1855." Lower Elwha Klallam Tribe. Last modified July 3, 2018. www.elwha.org/culture-history/point-no-point-treaty/.

Montler, Timothy. 2015. *Klallam Grammar.* Seattle, WA: University of Washington Press.

Radio Pacific, Inc. 2019. "Downtown Park to Be Renamed Pebble Beach Park." MyClallamCounty.com. Last modified March 19, 2019. www.myclallamcounty.com/2019/03/19/downtown-park-to-be-renamed-pebble-beach-park.

Valadez, Jamie. 2015. "Lower Elwha Klallam." In *Native Peoples of the Olympic Peninsula,* edited by Jacilee Wray. Norman, OK: University of Oklahoma Press.

Wray, Jacilee. 1997. *Olympic National Park: Ethnographic Overview Assessment.* Washington, DC: National Park Service.

# Contributors

**TIM MCNULTY** is a poet, essayist, and natural history writer. He is the author of three poetry collections and eleven books on natural history, including *Olympic National Park: A Natural History*. Tim has received the Washington State Book Award and the National Outdoor Book Award, among other honors. He's lived most of his life in the foothills of Washington's Olympic Mountains and serves on the board of Olympic Park Advocates, a conservation organization that focuses on the Olympic ecosystem. His website is timmcnultypoet.com.

**FAWN SHARP** serves as president of the National Congress of American Indians and is also the current vice president of the Quinault Indian Nation. She has dedicated her life to fighting to protect the sovereignty, human rights, and cultural inheritances of all Tribal Nations. A human rights attorney by training, she was recognized in 2018 by the United Nations as one of the foremost experts on the human rights of Indigenous people globally. After graduating from Gonzaga University, Fawn received her Juris Doctorate from the University of Washington and advanced certificates from the National Judicial College at the University of Nevada and the International Human Rights Law at Oxford University. She has held numerous leadership positions in both the Quinault Indian Nation and in Washington State, was vice president and a founding member for the National Intertribal Tax Alliance, and has sponsored climate change initiatives in Washington and beyond. While she lectures all over the United States, she continues to live on the Quinault Reservation in Taholah.

**DAVID GUTERSON** is the author of twelve books, including the novel *Snow Falling on Cedars* and the book-length poem *Turn Around Time*. As an inveterate walker and a Northwest native, he has hiked and climbed widely in the Olympic Mountains. Two of his novels—*The Other* and *Our Lady of the Forest*—are set on the Olympic Peninsula.

**WENDY SAMPSON** is a member of the Lower Elwha Klallam Tribe (LEKT); she lives on the reservation with her family. She has been a Klallam language teacher for twenty years. Her career began as a high school student hired to work with tribal elders as a teacher apprentice. After attending college she returned home and earned her Klallam language teacher certification in 2003 and eventually became the program manager. Wendy has provided cultural outreach in the schools, taught after-school programs and community adult classes, and worked under various grant projects with the goals of creating tribal history and language lessons and developing tools for language learning. She managed the LEKT Culture and Language program for ten years, overseeing the growth of the department and expansion of services until 2021. She is now a teacher for the Port Angeles School District offering courses in the Klallam language as well as history classes from a tribal perspective. Wendy remains dedicated to sharing her knowledge in an effort to continue revitalizing the Klallam language and culture in her community.

**LONI GRINNELL-GRENINGER** currently serves her people as the vice chairwoman at the Jamestown S'Klallam Tribe, beginning her service in January 2020. She graduated with her bachelor of science degree in psychology from Pacific Lutheran University in 2012, and her masters of public administration degree with an emphasis in Tribal Governance from The Evergreen State College in 2016. After spending four years working for the Washington State Department of Social & Health Services in Indian Policy and as a tribal liaison for behavioral health services, she came home to Jamestown to serve her people. She currently serves as the department director of Social & Community Services. In both of her roles, she works closely with federal, state, and local governments, as well as numerous tribal and non-tribal organizations to engage in policy and cultural work for her tribe and on behalf of Indian Country.

**GARY MORISHIMA** is a technical advisor in Natural Resources and Environment and former forest manager for the Quinault Indian Nation. He has a PhD in quantitative science and environmental management from the University of Washington, where he is an affiliate professor in the School of the Environment and Forest Sciences. He is a member of several Pacific Salmon Commission Technical Committees and a former member of the Salmon Technical Team of the Pacific Fishery Management Council. He also helped found the Intertribal Timber Council.

**MARIA PARKER PASCUA** (Hita·ʔa·ʔoƛ) is a Makah tribal member and lives in Neah Bay, Washington, where she teaches an online Makah language course through Peninsula College. She is a language specialist, Makah Language Program, at the Makah Cultural & Research Center Museum, a nonprofit charter organization of the Makah Tribe, and has her masters of education degree in Indigenous language revitalization from the University of Victoria. Her most recent publication, "Makah Language Dialogues," from Appendix B of her master's thesis in Indigenous language, was in response to COVID-19 isolation restrictions and the need to provide positive independent learning activities for adults in the Makah community. Besides her involvement in Makah song, dance, storytelling, weaving, and other cultural arts, she enjoys church and community activities, reading, writing, and music. She and her husband, Andrew, have five children and fourteen grandchildren.

**FRANCINE SWIFT** (Wah-wash-a-lee) is a member of the Port Gamble S'Klallam Tribe, a daughter of G. Jake and June Jones and granddaughter of Foster and Clara Jones and Wesley Jack and Gladys Brown. Francine is the mother of five children and grandmother to eighteen and a site manager for Northwest Indian College. A lifelong learner of academics and cultural teachings, Francine has had the privilege of serving her tribe as coordinator of longhouse carving and construction; she has also conducted oral interviews and compiled historical archives. Her father shared a lullaby, "Wah-wash-a-lee," that had been recorded on clay cylinders and she chose it as the name for herself, earning it by helping two families to prepare for a naming ceremony.

**JAMIE R. VALADEZ**, a Lower Elwha Klallam Tribal member, is a retired teacher of Klallam language and Native American history. Jamie is still active in the development of Klallam language teaching materials and currently working on a history of the Elwha Klallam Tribe. She also enjoys weaving baskets and is learning how to bead. As an elder of the tribe, she enjoys storytelling and providing cultural presentations.

**LYNDA V. MAPES** is an award-winning journalist, author, and close observer of the natural world. She is the author of six books, including *Orca: Shared Waters, Shared Home*; *Witness Tree: Seasons of Change in a Century Old Oak*; and *Elwha: A River Reborn*. Lynda lives in Seattle where she covers nature, the environment, and tribes as a staff reporter for *The Seattle Times*.

# Photo Credits

## Photography by John Gussman with Pat O'Hara, Gemina Garland-Lewis, Larry Workman, Art Wolfe

*and* Byron Adams, William Baccus, Paul Bannick, Janis Burger, Bryant Carlin, Rob Casey, Brandon Cole, Lucas Cometto, Steve Grace, Amy Gulick, David Herasimtschuk, Benji Ives, Eirik Johnson, Steven Kazlowski, Brett Lovelace, Glenn Nelson, Wendy Sampson, Douglas Scott, Dave Shreffler, George Sternberg, Dan Sullivan, Francine Swift, Gerrit Vyn, Richard Walker, and Kiliii Yuyan.

### PHOTO CREDITS

**Byron A. Adams**: page 161 (bottom)

**Paul Bannick**: pages 78 (left), 159, 163

**John Bornsworth/Peninsula Environment**: page 139

**Janis Burger**: pages 45, 47, 49 (top left and right), 119, 121 (top left and bottom left), 169 (right), 173 (top center)

**Bryant Carlin**: pages 43, 49 (bottom left)

**Rob Casey**: pages 99 (top), 122 (top right), 127

**Brandon Cole**: pages 98 (right), 116 (bottom left), 123

**Lucas Cometto**: page 59

**Asahel Curtis**, courtesy Olympic National Park: page 161

**Gemina Garland-Lewis**: pages 38 (top), 48 (top), 82 (top right), 83, 87, 89, 126, 130–131, 136, 137, 146, 147, 168 (right)

**Steve Grace**: pages 39, 118 (right), 121 (right), 122 (left and bottom right), 172 (top left and bottom left), 173 (top left and top right), 196–197

**Amy Gulick**: pages 33, 34–35, 116 (top)

**John Gussman**: pages 1, 2, 6–7, 8–9, 10–11, 20–21, 28–29, 50, 57, 58, 60, 61, 62–63, 72, 76–77, 79 (bottom right), 92, 93, 94 (top right), 97, 98 (left), 99, 100, 101, 112, 115, 116 (bottom right), 117, 120, 125, 128, 129, 138, 142, 152, 166–167, 168 (top left), 172 (top right), 173 (bottom), 174–175, 190, 191, 193, 198, 207, back cover

**David Herasimtschuk**: pages 12–13, 90, 208

**Benji Ives**: pages 178 (top right), 179 (left)

**Eirik Johnson**: pages 24, 132

**Steven Kazlowski**: pages 27, 37, 64, 82 (bottom left), 102–103, 154, 168 (bottom), 192

**Brett Lovelace/ Oregon State University**: page 158

**Molly Neely-Walker**: page 178

**Glenn Nelson**: pages 38 (bottom), 171

**Pat O'Hara**: pages 3, 4, 23, 46, 48 (bottom left, bottom right), 51, 52, 53, 68, 69, 70–71, 75, 82 (bottom right), 84–85, 135, 144, 170

Courtesy **Olympic National Park**: page 162

Courtesy **Port Gamble S'Klallam Tribe**: pages 176, 177

**Wendy Sampson**: pages 148–149, 151

**Douglas Scott**: pages 44, 86, 182–183, 184, 185

**Dave Shreffler**: pages 32, 67, 164, 187, 188, 189

**George Sternberg**: page 145

**Dan Sullivan/NPS**: page 55

**Francine Swift**: pages 179 (top right and bottom right), 180

**Gerrit Vyn**: pages 78 (right), 79 (top left, top right, and bottom left), 94 (top left and bottom), 95, 96, 113

**Richard Walker**: page 178 (top left and bottom)

Courtesy **Washington Department of Fish and Wildlife**: page 165

**Art Wolfe**: front cover and pages 5, 30–31, 107, 118 (left), 124, 140–141, 157, 169 (left), 194–195, 206

**Larry Workman**: pages 14, 15, 16, 17, 40–41, 82 (top left), 111, 143, 153, 155, 156, 160, 172 (top right)

**Kiliii Yuyan**: pages 104, 108, 110

# Resources

*Use these resources to search, learn more about, and experience the Olympic Peninsula. This list continues to be updated on the book's website: www.SalmonCedar.org*

**PUBLIC LANDS**
Dungeness National Wildlife Refuge
Bogachiel State Park
Dosewallips State Park
Fort Townsend Historical State Park
Fort Worden Historical State Park
Miller Peninsula State Park
Olympic Coast National Marine Sanctuary
Olympic National Forest
Olympic National Park
Sequim Bay State Park
Triton Cove State Park
Washington Islands National
   Wildlife Refuges

**TRIBES**
Hoh Tribe
Jamestown S'Klallam Tribe
Lower Elwha Klallam Tribe
Makah Tribe
Port Gamble S'Klallam Tribe
Quileute Tribe
Quinault Indian Nation
Skokomish Indian Tribes

**COMMUNITIES**
Forks Chamber of Commerce
Greater Kingston Community Chamber
   of Commerce
Greater Kitsap Chamber of Commerce
Jefferson County Chamber of Commerce
North Hood Canal Chamber of Commerce
Neah Bay Chamber of Commerce
Port Angeles Chamber of Commerce
Sequim Chamber of Commerce
Westport-Grayland Chamber
   of Commerce

**CONSERVATION PARTNERS**
American Rivers
American Whitewater
Big City Mountaineers
Clallam Conservation District
Conservation Northwest
Friends of Olympic National Park
Leave No Trace Center for Outdoor Ethics
The Mountaineers
National Forest Foundation
National Outdoor Leadership School
National Parks Conservation Association
Olympic Coast National Marine Sanctuary
Peninsula Wilderness Club
Pew Trust
Save Our Wild Salmon
Save the Olympic Peninsula
Seattle Audubon Society
Streamkeepers
The Student Conservation Association
Trout Unlimited
Washington Coast Savers
Washington Trails Association
Washington's National Park Fund

**EDUCATION ORGANIZATIONS**
Coastal Interpretive Center
   (Ocean Shores)
Dungeness River Nature Center
NatureBridge (Lake Crescent)
Olympic Natural Resources Center (Forks)

**LAND TRUSTS**
Jefferson Land Trust North
The Nature Conservancy
Olympic Land Trust

**MARINE CENTERS**
Feiro Marine Life Center
Marine Discovery Center (Port Angeles)
Port Townsend Marine Science Center

**MUSEUMS**
Burke Museum of Natural and
   Cultural History
The Carnegie (Elwha Klallam Museum at
   the Carnegie)
Forks Timber Museum
Jefferson Museum of Art & History
Makah Cultural & Research
   Center Museum
Port Gamble Historic Museum
Quilcene Historical Museum
Quinault Cultural Center and Museum
Sequim Museum & Arts

**RESTORATION ORGANIZATIONS**
Coastal Watershed Institute
Dungeness River Management Team
Hood Canal Watershed Council
North Olympic Salmon Coalition
Northwest Watershed Institute
Skokomish Watershed Action Team

# BRAIDED RIVER

BRAIDED RIVER, the conservation imprint of Mountaineers Books, combines photography and writing to bring a fresh perspective to key environmental issues facing western North America's wildest places. Our books reach beyond the printed page as we take these distinctive voices and vision to a wider audience through lectures, exhibits, and multimedia events. Our goal is to build public support for wilderness preservation campaigns and inspire public action. This work is made possible through the book sales and contributions made to Braided River, a 501(c)(3) nonprofit organization. Please visit BraidedRiver.org for more information on events, exhibits, speakers, and how to contribute to this work.

Braided River books may be purchased for corporate, educational, or other promotional sales. For special discounts and information, contact our sales department at 800.553.4453 or mbooks@mountaineersbooks.org.

THE MOUNTAINEERS, founded in 1906, is a nonprofit outdoor activity and conservation organization, whose mission is "to explore, study, preserve, and enjoy the natural beauty of the outdoors." Mountaineers Books supports this mission by publishing travel and natural history guides, instructional texts, and works on conservation and history.

See our website to explore our catalog of over 700 outdoor titles:
Mountaineers Books
1001 SW Klickitat Way, Suite 201
Seattle, WA 98134
800.553.4453
www.mountaineersbooks.org

FSC
MIX
Paper | Supporting
responsible forestry
FSC® C008047
www.fsc.org

For more information, visit www.SalmonCedar.org

Printed in China on FSC®-certified paper using soy-based ink.
26  25  24  23     1  2  3  4  5

Executive Director, Braided River, and Photo Editor: Helen Cherullo
Braided River Deputy Director: Erika Lundhal
Editor in Chief: Kate Rogers
Project Editor: Mary Metz
Copyeditor: Sarah Currin
Cover and Book Designer: Kate Basart/Union Pageworks
Cartographer: Erin Greb

**Page 1:** *A short, accessible walk from the Elwha River leads to scenic Madison Falls on Madison Creek. Olympic National Park.*
**Page 2:** *Rarest of Olympic salmon, sockeye spawn in large lakes such as Lake Quinault and Ozette Lake.* **Page 3:** *Western redcedar, a foundational species for Northwest Coast cultures and western hemlock: two iconic trees of the Olympic rain forest.* **Page 4:** *A short hike from Anderson Pass leads to this post–ice age landscape in Olympic National Park.* **Page 5:** *Maple trees reflected in Sol Duc River, Olympic National Park. Title pages: Sol Duc Falls, one of the most popular old-growth forest hikes in Olympic National Park.* **Page 206:** *The Milky Way streams over Point of the Arches and Shi Shi Beach in Olympic National Park.* **Page 207:** *A winter view of the lower Elwha Valley looks toward the cloud-covered Olympic Mountains.* **Page 208:** *Juvenile Chinook salmon take cover under a large fallen log on the Elwha River.*

Library of Congress Cataloging-in-Publication data is on file for this title

ISBN: 978-1-68051-529-9